Crown Jewels

Crown Jewels

Five Great National Parks
Around the World and the Challenges They Face

Edited by Randolph Delehanty, Ph.D.

 **The AAM Press**

American Alliance of Museums
Washington, D.C.
2013

Dedication

To my colleagues at the Presidio Trust, Golden Gate National Recreation Area, and Golden Gate National Parks Conservancy.

— Randolph Delehanty

Cover page: **A colorful Great Barrier Reef scene** of small fish swimming over soft tree corals, feather stars, and Tubastraea corals with some yellow tentacles extended.
R. & V. Taylor © Commonwealth of Australia (GBRMPA)

Pages v-vi: In a class all by itself is the **spectacular migration of mammals** (mainly, wildebeest and zebras) that passes through the Serengeti Park in the thousands late in the year, often accompanied by hungry predators.
Photo by Robert W. Floerke

Following pages: An **expedition traversing the northern Chang Tang**, Tibet, at elevations above 16,000 feet in November 2006. In the first 1,000 miles of roadless travel, the author and his companions encountered no people.
Photo by George B. Schaller

Crown Jewels
Five Great National Parks Around the World and the Challenges They Face

Edited by Randolph Delehanty, Ph.D.

Published by The AAM Press of the American Alliance of Museums, 1575 Eye St., N.W., Suite 400, Washington, DC, 20005, www.aam-us.org
Publisher, John Strand
Designed by Susan v. Levine, creative director

ISBN 978-1-933253-73-2

Crown jewels : five great national parks around the world and the challenges they face / edited by Randolph Delehanty.
     pages cm
  Includes index.
  ISBN 978-1-933253-73-2 (print)
  ISBN 978-1-933253-81-7 (e-book)

1. National parks and reserves--Conservation and restoration. 2. Nature conservation. I. Delehanty, Randolph, editor of compilation.
  SB481.C76 2013
  363.6'8--dc23
                              2013001225

Contents

xii   Preface

2   Introduction

9   U.S. National Parks and Protected Areas: Past, Present, and Future
RANDOLPH DELEHANTY, PH.D. / PRESIDIO TRUST, SAN FRANCISCO

51   Chang Tang Nature Reserve, China
Nature Reserves, Wildlife, and Pastoralists in Tibet
GEORGE B. SCHALLER, PH.D. / WILDLIFE CONSERVATION SOCIETY, NEW YORK

71   Serengeti National Park and Ngorongoro Conservation Area, Tanzania
Prospects, Problems, and Progress
JOHN F. R. BOWER, PH.D. / UNIVERSITY OF CALIFORNIA, DAVIS, AND AUDAX Z. MABULLA / UNIVERSITY OF DAR ES SALAAM, TANZANIA

83   National Archeological Parks of Pompeii, Herculaneum, Stabiae, Boscoreale, and Oplontis, Italy
Mass Tourism, Pleasures, and Politics in the Shadow of Vesuvius
JUDITH HARRIS / ROME

99   Alto Orinoco-Casiquiare Biosphere Reserve, Venezuela, and Yanomami Territory, Brazil
National Reserves and the Yanomami People in the Amazonian Rainforest
FIONA WATSON AND JOANNA EEDE / SURVIVAL INTERNATIONAL, LONDON

119   Great Barrier Reef Marine Park, Australia
National Parks, Changes in Perception, and Hyper-Reality
CELMARA POCOCK, PH.D. / UNIVERSITY OF SOUTHERN QUEENSLAND, AUSTRALIA

139   Changes in the Scientific Understanding of Nature
Can National Parks Be Preserved "Unimpaired"?
RANDOLPH DELEHANTY, PH.D. / PRESIDIO TRUST

144   Appendix
The International Union for Conservation of Nature and Natural Resources
Definitions of Protected Areas

146   Contributors

152   Index

Preface

Craig Middleton,
Executive Director, The Presidio Trust

The Presidio Trust is proud to present *Crown Jewels: Five Great National Parks Around the World and the Challenges They Face*. We hope that this book and the exhibition it is based on raise awareness about the myriad forms that parks take around the world, and also stimulate an important conversation regarding the pressing challenges they face in the 21st century.

Here at the Presidio in San Francisco, the Trust faced a two-fold challenge—to steward one of our nation's oldest military posts as it was transformed to serve a new purpose, and to sustain it as the country's first financially self-sufficient national park site. Working with our key partners, the National Park Service and the Golden Gate National Parks Conservancy, as well as countless community members and organizations, we achieved the milestone of financial self-sufficiency in 2013. At this point we provide one example for how a small but significant site can meet its essential challenge and be protected and sustained in innovative ways.

As we write the next chapter of the Presidio's history, we are committed to continuing a tradition of national service that began here centuries ago when this former military post served under the flags of Spain, Mexico, and finally the United States. During those long centuries, the Presidio always had impacts that extended far beyond its walls. Today the Presidio Trust strives to have a positive social impact by addressing some of the unique challenges we face today. This book and exhibit are part of our effort to do that.

Please join us in a conversation about the contemporary role parks play in a global context, the challenges of stewarding cherished public lands today, and the innovations that will sustain them tomorrow. Let us be inspired by these five great national parks, and together we can preserve them and many more.

Right: **In pursuit of water** for their livestock, Maasai herders have inadvertently destroyed evidence of human prehistory at fragile archeological sites.
Photo © Carol Beckwith/ photokunst

Introduction

Randolph Delehanty, Ph.D.
Historian, Presidio Trust, San Francisco

The national park idea emerged in 1872 with the establishment of Yellowstone by U.S. President Ulysses S. Grant. Today there are at least 7,000 national parks around the globe in 140 countries. But just as nation-states differ greatly, so does the management of their national parks. The International Union of Conservation of Nature advises UNESCO on natural sites, and its World Commission on Protected Areas provides the official definitions of a protected area (see Appendix 1). Paris-based UNESCO also lists world heritage sites, which now number 911. UNESCO has also established 580 Biosphere Reserves around the world. If we include protected areas beyond national parks, such as biological reserves and marine sanctuaries, the world's total number of protected areas zooms to 100,000. Collectively, they protect about 13 percent of the Earth's land but only about one-half percent of its oceans.

But even as protected areas have increased in number and extent, biological diversity has decreased worldwide. Humans directly affect about 83 percent of the Earth's land and all of its atmosphere and oceans. Close to one third of the Earth's land surface has been permanently altered by humans for agriculture and settlements. This has put great pressure on many ecosystems. The United Nations estimates that an additional one-third of lands could be altered in the next 100 years. According to the World Resources Institute, in 2002 protected areas ranged from about 11.1 percent of North America to only 2.1 percent of North Africa and the Middle East. Protected areas are important to species conservation and regeneration. Aquatic species such as tuna, sharks, seals, whales, and sea turtles that forage over entire oceans require protection of more than just their breeding areas. Protected areas are a vast subject; to my knowledge, there is no systematic, global overview of all national parks and protected areas.

Because the United States had the earliest and one of the best developed national park systems, this book begins with the story of the growth and development of the National Park System and other protected areas in the U.S. We then turn to five important parks around the globe—in East Africa, southern Italy, Amazonia, Tibet, and Australia—to examine the challenges they face.

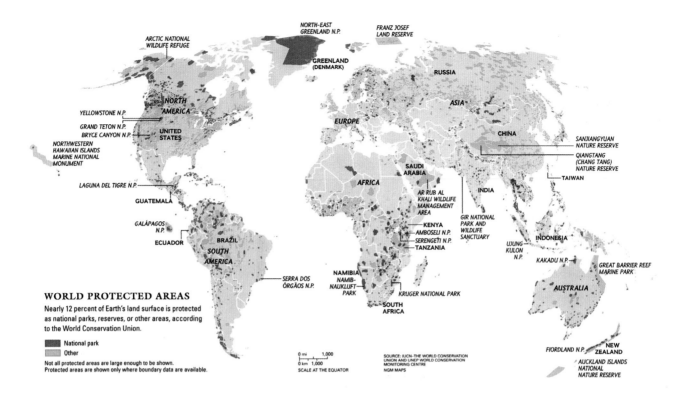

WORLD PROTECTED AREAS

Nearly 12 percent of Earth's land surface is protected as national parks, reserves, or other areas, according to the World Conservation Union.

■ National park
□ Other

Not all protected areas are large enough to be shown.
Protected areas are shown only where boundary data are available.

0 mi 1,000
0 km 1,000
SCALE AT THE EQUATOR

SOURCE: IUCN–THE WORLD CONSERVATION
UNION AND UNEP WORLD CONSERVATION
MONITORING CENTRE
NGM MAPS

Above: **World Protected Areas**, *National Geographic*, October 2006.

These parks were selected to show the variety of protected areas—natural and cultural, terrestrial and aquatic, old and recent—and the different kinds of challenges they face. Each park is analyzed by an expert with a lifetime's work in that part of the world. While all parks now face the challenge of global warming and other environmental threats, each nation and each of these particular national parks faces specific challenges. This book aims to show the importance of protected areas and the complexity and uncertainty of their individual and collective futures.

The first chapter sketches the evolution of national parks and protected areas in the United States and concludes with their present-day challenges, some of which are particular to the U.S. and others, such as climate change, that impact parks around the world.

The creation of parks and protected areas in the U.S. is not an ever-ascending, straight-line development. Parks and protected areas are political and economic creations, and shifts in politics and economies have always been important in their creation and management. National

parks are not the only protected lands and waters in the U.S. The U.S. Forest Service and other federal agencies with a conservation mandate are also responsible for large land holdings. The complex, even convoluted relationships among separate conservation agencies, principally in the Department of the Interior, but also in the Department of Agriculture and the Department of Commerce, are critically important in the politics of preservation and conservation. The history of the often antagonistic relationship between the U.S. Forest Service and the National Park Service is only the best known of these bureaucratic struggles. Today private land conservation easements are expanding the number of protected areas in the U.S. in a less visible but important way.

The Serengeti National Park (founded in 1951) and the adjoining Ngorongoro Conservation Area Authority (1959) in northern Tanzania protect not only the greatest concentration of wildlife in the world, but also paleoanthropological sites such as Olduvai Gorge with its hominid fossils and 3.6 million-year-old footprints, which are of central importance in the understanding of human biological and

Exploiting and Protecting Land

Humans have altered great swaths of the planet for agriculture and settlements, putting extreme pressure on many ecosystems. Close to a third of the world's land surface has been converted for human use. The United Nations estimates that an additional one-third of lands could be converted in the next 100 years. Far less land is protected from development.

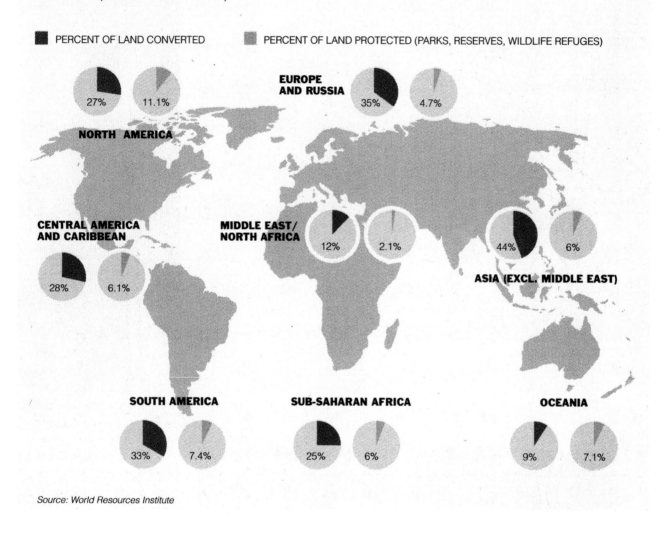

■ PERCENT OF LAND CONVERTED   ■ PERCENT OF LAND PROTECTED (PARKS, RESERVES, WILDLIFE REFUGES)

NORTH AMERICA — 27% / 11.1%

EUROPE AND RUSSIA — 35% / 4.7%

CENTRAL AMERICA AND CARIBBEAN — 28% / 6.1%

MIDDLE EAST/ NORTH AFRICA — 12% / 2.1%

ASIA (EXCL. MIDDLE EAST) — 44% / 6%

SOUTH AMERICA — 33% / 7.4%

SUB-SAHARAN AFRICA — 25% / 6%

OCEANIA — 9% / 7.1%

Source: World Resources Institute

cultural origins. While the Serengeti is a wildlife reserve and a world-famous tourist destination, the adjoining Ngorongoro is a multiple-use area where the Maasai people live and herd cattle. Scientific, philanthropic, environmental, indigenous, and tourism interests see these adjoining fragile areas in conflicting ways. Tanzania's protected areas face great economic, educational, legislative, jurisdictional, policing, and cultural management challenges. Expanding tourist facilities, gravel quarries, roads, and dams threaten Tanzania's natural and cultural heritage. And in this case, it is not just one

nation's inheritance that is at risk, but humanity's cradle itself. To damage the paleoanthropological record in East Africa is to erase important evidence of human evolution that belongs not just to this generation, but to all humankind into the unbounded future. For who knows what our future scientists will be able to tell us about our past?

Vesuvius National Park in Campagna, Italy, protects the famous volcano, though illegal building continues on its slopes. Nearby are the premier archeological parks of Herculaneum and

Converted and Protected Land by Region.
New York Times / World Resources Institute, 2002.

Pompeii. Pompeii is the largest excavated archeological site from classical Western antiquity. Excavations began there in the 1740s and parts of the site have been exposed to the elements for over 260 years. Some 2.4 million tourists tramp through the fragile ruins every year. All the Vesuvian sites are state-owned, and all suffer from problems in the accountability of funds and understaffing. They are cultural islands within territories dominated by the Neapolitan crime syndicates of the Camorra. The newest challenges they face are political interference in, and commercial exploitation of, these irreplaceable treasures of humankind's cultural heritage. Illegal toxic waste dumping also threatens the park.

The Yanomami are the largest relatively isolated tribe in South America. Numbering about 32,000 people, they live in the Amazonian rainforest straddling the borders of southern Venezuela and northern Brazil. They hunt game animals; fish; gather wild fruits, nuts, shellfish, and insect larvae; as well as grow crops in forest gardens. In Venezuela, the Yanomami live in the Alto Orinoco-Casiquiare Biosphere Reserve (20.7 million acres), which was established in 1991. In Brazil, the Yanomami live in a territory about the same size as Portugal (23.2 million acres), formally recognized in 1992. The combined area inhabited by the Yanomami is the largest indigenous territory in a tropical rainforest anywhere in the world.

Roads and military outposts are putting pressure on the Yanomami and their land. They also face serious threats from introduced diseases, as well as violence and environmental degradation at the hands of gold miners who are invading their land. There are several Yanomami-run organizations established to defend and advocate for their rights, to protect their lands, and to strengthen their culture. Survival International in London, a nonprofit organization that helps tribal peoples defend their lives, protect their lands, and determine their own futures, in collaboration with the Yanomami, is campaigning for Venezuela and Brazil to implement effective land protection in Amazonia.

The Chang Tang Nature Reserve, established in 1993 on the Tibetan plateau, is a vast, high-altitude, arid steppe in the northwestern part of the Tibetan Autonomous Region of China. Three other reserves adjoin it: the Kekexili Reserve in Qinghai Province established in 1995, the Mid-Kunlun Reserve in Xinjiang (2001), and the West Kunlun Nature Reserve (2006). Together they embrace 175,000 square miles of ecosystem and provide protection for wildlife, including several endangered species: the Tibetan gazelle, wild yak, wolf, snow leopard, the Tibetan brown bear, and Tibetan antelope or chiru. These reserves are multiple-use areas and are home to nomadic pastoralists. But as Tibet develops rapidly, the communal grazing areas are being parceled out and the number of nomads and their livestock herds are increasing, resulting in fence-building and conflict with migrating wildlife. Poaching of chiru for their meat, horns, and fine wool is also a serious problem. Fostering sustainable economic development for nomadic people while protecting biodiversity and wildlife is critical in remote Tibet, one third of which is now under protected reserve status.

The Great Barrier Reef Marine Park Authority in Queensland, Australia, was established in 1975. It manages one of the largest living things on Earth. Invasive species, climate change, and agricultural

Following page: **The Great Barrier Reef tank** at the Sydney Aquarium, where "you get a 360-degree view of all the goings-on in the busy world of the Great Barrier Reef."
© Andrea Re Depaolini (www.flickr.com/photos/plur44)

runoff threaten this spectacular coral reef. A less well-known kind of degradation is taking place in popular perception. Direct sensuous experience of the Reef is being replaced by substitutes that can seem more authentic than the Reef itself. Visitors to the islands and reefs once enjoyed embodied encounters—touch, sound, sight, smell, and taste combined in an oriented experience—that created a strong sense of place. As visitor experiences become increasingly shaped by media, imagination, technology, and conservation, visitors are becoming distanced from the Reef's unique environment. Despite unprecedented access to the underwater, tourists are now more likely to experience the Reef through secondary visual representations rather than the Reef itself. Also, the natural environment is being altered to match tourists' expectation of a Tahiti-like setting by the planting of palm trees and other flora where they do not occur naturally. At the Great Barrier Reef we witness the paradox of a park attracting people who then want to change the place to fit their touristic preconceptions.

Each of the chapters illustrates and digs deeper into specific challenges. The cumulative effect, I hope, is that the reader achieves both a deeper understanding of what national parks are, how they were created and are sustained, what challenges they face, and what all who care for them can do. At the end of each chapter is a short list of key books and websites where you can learn more, and organizations and governmental agencies you can contact to advocate for responsible stewardship. While different nation-states administer these parks and reserves, these magnificent places really belong to all of us. And their future depends on all of us, as well.

U.S. National Parks and Protected Areas: Past, Present, and Future

Randolph Delehanty, Ph.D.
Historian, Presidio Trust, San Francisco

Federal and Tribal Lands and National Parks in the United States

The national park idea, a major contribution by the United States of America to world culture, did not emerge full-blown in 1872 at Yellowstone, Wyoming. National parks have evolved over many generations through a series of ideological, political, economic, scientific, and managerial changes. As the modern world around them changes, the national parks have had to change as well. Among their greatest challenges, as we will see, are the profound impact that global climate change, air pollution, and other ecological threats are having on them. Simultaneously, fundamental shifts in philosophy are replacing the old assumption that ecosystems are relatively stable and static and seek equilibrium, and that scientific certainty is possible. There is a new realization of the inherent uncertainty and unpredictability of ecological change. This new thinking is changing park philosophy, policy, and management. Much of the public is not yet aware of this fundamental intellectual shift.

The national park idea emerged within a larger context that included the invention of scenic municipal parks, utilitarian forest management, major changes in transportation and recreation, important advances in scientific and ecological thought and practice, as well as fundamental changes in the organization and roles of the departments of the federal government. In a country with an ideology of limited government and a history favoring the transfer of the public domain to private ownership and exploitation, the creation of and continued support for parks and reserves have been an unending political struggle.

The United States has a total land area of nearly 2.3 billion acres. Of that, the federal government owns nearly 650 million acres, 28 percent of the nation, more than a third of which is in Alaska. As of 2002, about 13.1 percent of the total land area of the U.S. was protected in parks and wildlife areas. Four federal departments manage public lands and waters, each under its own secretary in the president's cabinet. Within the Department of the Interior are the National Park Service, responsible for 84 million acres and at least 27,000 historic structures and more than 68,000 archeological sites; the Bureau of Land Management that manages 253 million acres of public land in the West and Alaska; the U.S. Fish and Wildlife Service that manages 553 national wildlife refuges,

Left: **Bryce Canyon National Park, Utah**.
iStock photo by SabrinaPintus

66 national fish hatcheries, and 37 wetland districts covering 150 million acres; and the Bureau of Reclamation with 7.1 million acres. Under the Bureau of Indian Affairs in Interior are approximately 310 Indian reservations governed by tribes, embracing a total of 55.7 million acres, about 2.3 percent of the area of the U.S. Nine reservations are larger than Delaware. The largest is the Navajo Reservation, with 16 million acres, about the size of West Virginia. Many smaller reservations are less than 1,000 acres, and the smallest are less than 100 acres. Within the Department of Agriculture is the U.S. Forest Service that manages 155 national forests and 20 national grasslands encompassing a total of 193 million acres. Within the Department of Commerce is the National Oceanic and Atmospheric Administration that manages 14 national marine sanctuaries totaling 150,000 sq. miles. The Department of Defense holds 29 million acres in military reservations, which are subject to a Natural Resources Conservation Compliance Program. All these federal and tribal lands can be viewed at www.nationalatlas.gov.

Protected Areas in the United States
See graph facing page.
1. DEPARTMENT OF THE INTERIOR

National Park Service manages 84 million acres in 58 national parks and 334 other properties. (Alaska accounts for two-thirds of all national park land.)

There are 20 different categories of natural, historical, recreational, and cultural "units" managed by the National Park Service, including at least 27,000 historic structures and more than 68,000 archeological sites.

Bureau of Land Management manages 253 million acres of public land in the West and Alaska.

U.S. Fish and Wildlife Service that manages 553 national wildlife refuges, 66 national fish hatcheries, and 37 wetland districts covering 150 million acres.

Bureau of Reclamation manages 7.1 million acres of land for irrigation and power generation.

Bureau of Indian Affairs
About 310 reservations under tribal governments hold 55.7 million acres.

2. DEPARTMENT OF AGRICULTURE

U.S. Forest Service that manages 155 national forests and 20 national grasslands encompassing a total of 193 million acres.

3. DEPARTMENT OF COMMERCE

National Oceanic and Atmospheric Administration manages 14 national marine sanctuaries totaling 150,000 square miles.

4. DEPARTMENT OF DEFENSE

Military reservations total 29 million acres of land and waters.

5. STATE PARKS

State parks (excluding county and municipal parks) embrace more than 13 million acres.
There are also uncounted state-owned historic sites.

California was long the national leader in state parks, with 278 parks totaling 1.4 million acres. This includes almost one-third of the state's scenic coastline, or 280 miles.

6. PRIVATE LAND TRUSTS (CONSERVATION EASEMENTS)

There are 47 million acres in state, local, and national land trusts.

Protected Areas in the United States
in Millions of Acres by Agency plus Private Land Trusts

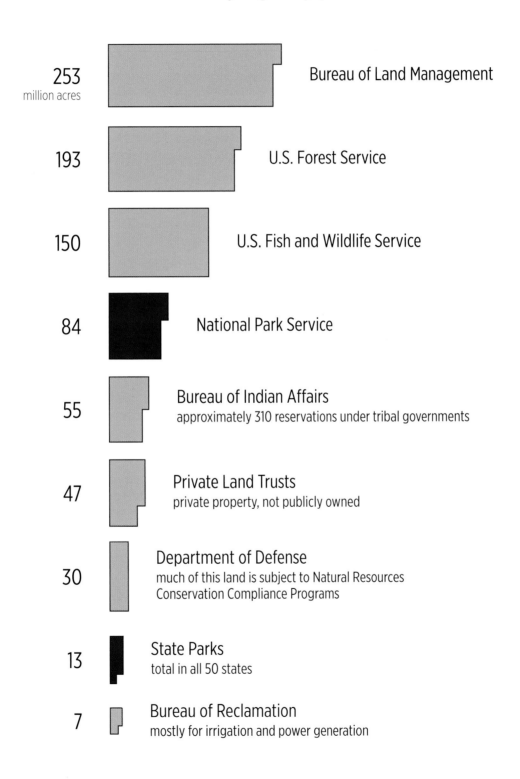

253 million acres — Bureau of Land Management

193 — U.S. Forest Service

150 — U.S. Fish and Wildlife Service

84 — National Park Service

55 — Bureau of Indian Affairs
approximately 310 reservations under tribal governments

47 — Private Land Trusts
private property, not publicly owned

30 — Department of Defense
much of this land is subject to Natural Resources Conservation Compliance Programs

13 — State Parks
total in all 50 states

7 — Bureau of Reclamation
mostly for irrigation and power generation

1 million acres = 404,686 hectares

THE NATIONAL PARK SYSTEM

MAP KEY

National Park System

Affiliated area

A map of the National
Trails System appears on
pages 520 and 521.

Today there are 20 different categories of natural, historical, recreational, and cultural "units" managed by the National Park Service. By 2009, the National Park Service managed 58 national parks and 334 other properties from the Washington Monument on the National Mall to the Statue of Liberty and the Selma to Montgomery National Historic Trail. In 2010, there were 21,574 National Park Service employees and the NPS budget was $3.16 billion. The future portends flat, or shrinking, congressional appropriations for national parks.

The Crisis in State Parks

In addition to federal parks and reserves, there are also state park systems, as well as county and municipal parks across the country. Collectively, state parks (excluding county and municipal parks) embrace more than 13 million acres. There are also uncounted state-owned historic sites. Budgets for many state parks and historic

sites have been under pressure in recent years. By 2010, 26 states had already closed parks, limited hours, reduced staff or budgets, or deferred maintenance.

California was long the national leader in state parks with 278 parks totaling 1.4 million acres. This includes almost one-third of the state's scenic coastline, or 280 miles. The first state park was the California Redwood Park in Big Basin, Santa Cruz County, founded in 1902. The largest is Anza-Borrego Desert State Park with 470,000 acres in San Diego County, established in 1933. The California State Park Commission was organized in 1927, and the first park bond act passed by three-to-one the following year. California state park units include underwater preserves, nature reserves, parks, beaches, recreation areas, campgrounds, wilderness areas, ancient sites, historic buildings, lighthouses, ghost towns, conference centers, the spectacular Hearst Castle (which is income-producing), and eight

The National Park System in the United States. Mel White, *Complete National Parks of the United States*, Washington, D.C.: National Geographic Society, 2009

off-highway vehicle parks for motorcycles and all-terrain vehicles.

The California Department of Parks and Recreation budget has been reduced by a third in recent years. In 2012, the state park budget was $384 million and the maintenance backlog totaled $1.3 billion. Republican California Governor Arnold Schwarzenegger proposed closing 220 parks, leaving only 59 parks. Though that did not happen, budgets and staff were cut and partial closures were imposed. In 2012, Democratic Governor Jerry Brown proposed closing 54 of the 278 state parks in order to save $22 million. In the end, only two parks were closed, but no long-term funding solution has been found. The future seems to portend allowing local governments and nonprofit organizations to manage some state parks. While California's chronic budgetary crisis attracts national attention, other states are also cutting back on their parks. In 2010, The National Trust for Historic Preservation put *all* state parks and state-owned historic sites on its list of the most endangered historic places.[1]

Private Protected Lands and Land Trusts

Sixty percent of the land in the U.S. is privately owned. Perhaps the least well-known efforts to expand protected areas are taking place on privately owned land. Today, there are significant *private* land conservation efforts in addition to the work of government entities. Land trusts that accept conservation easements in perpetuity are growing in importance as public funds for acquiring parklands dwindle and as land costs escalate. The Land Trust Alliance was founded in 1982 to promote and coordinate these individual, private efforts. The Alliance conducts the National Land Trust Census and lists lands protected by state, local, and national land trusts. The last census in 2010 reported that private land trusts protect 47 million acres of land in the U.S., double that recorded in the 2000 land trust census.

Artist George Catlin's Vision / Hot Springs National Reservation

The first call for a national park in the United States came from George Catlin (1796–1872), the artist and ethnographer of the Plains Indians. In 1832, contemplating the reeking carcasses of bison slaughtered for their tongues and the intoxicated Sioux in South Dakota, he climbed a bluff and meditated on "the deadly axe and desolating hand of cultivating man." Then he imagined "by some great protecting policy of the government" the creation of "a magnificent park ... a *nation's Park*, containing man and beast, in all the wild and freshness of their nature's beauty...." He envisioned a vast reserve from the plains to the Rocky Mountains and from Canada to Mexico. Nothing came of his radical vision.

In 1832, Congress protected a natural feature for the first time, establishing the Hot Springs National Reservation in Arkansas signed into law by President Andrew Jackson. But that timid precedent was not taken any further as the nation expanded rapidly westward. Before the income tax, land sales were an important part of federal revenue, and doing a "land office business" became a byword for brisk sales. Almost no one thought of reserving parts of the public domain.

The Negative Lesson of Niagara Falls

In the 1830s, Niagara Falls on the border of New York State and Canada was the chief scenic wonder in the new United

States. Americans and Europeans flocked to see and hear the thundering cataract, the most powerful waterfall in North America. But when they got there what they experienced was a privatized landscape where they had to pay to see the falls and where commercial clutter spoiled the view. Neither the federal nor the state government had had the foresight to reserve the falls for public enjoyment. Instead, the choice rim lots were sold off for private exploitation, and hydroelectric companies threatened to divert the river and impair the flow of water. European travelers were scathing in their comments and thoughtful Americans were embarrassed. Artist Frederic Edwin Church, landscape designer Frederick Law Olmsted, architect Henry Hobson Richardson, and others formed Free Niagara to urge conservation of the falls. In 1879, New York State commissioned Olmsted and James T. Gardner to survey the falls. In 1882, The Niagara Falls Association, a citizens' group, organized a petition drive in support of a park. New York Governor David B. Hill signed legislation in 1885 creating the Niagara Reservation State Park, and the state began to purchase land. In 1887, Olmsted and Calvert Vaux created a plan "to restore and conserve the natural surroundings of the Falls of Niagara, rather than to attempt to add anything thereto." A treaty between the U.S. and Canada regulated water diversion in 1909 (revised in 1950). Today, up to three fourths of the flow can be diverted at night and during non-tourist season for power generation.

Urbanization and Man-Made Scenic Parks

In the mid-19th century, as European and American cities grew explosively with railroads, industrialization, population growth, and mass immigration, city dwellers could no longer easily escape to nearby country for recreation. Visionary, elite reformers persuaded municipal governments to buy marginal land and to develop large landscaped parks accessible to wealthy and middle-class city dwellers. These new parks were artificial scenic creations inspired by the Romantic landscape tradition of the great aristocratic estates of England. The new parks provided places for passive recreation but not active sports. Frederick Law Olmsted, one of the early promoters and designers of these parks, argued that harried businessmen needed calming places to relax their over-wrought nerves. Birkenhead Park in Liverpool (1843–47), Central Park in New York (1859), Parc Buttes de Chaumont in Paris (1867), and Golden Gate Park in San Francisco (1871) are among the best known of these elaborate, costly, man-made creations that brought cultivated nature to major cities.

The First National Parks: Yosemite in 1864 and Yellowstone in 1872

After the conquest of Mexico in 1846–48 and the cession of California and the Southwest, the United States was suddenly in possession of a sparsely populated public domain of enormous extent. Certain places in this vast territory were scenic wonders far more extensive and dramatic than anything east of the Mississippi River. The United States now had places that outshone the Old World's Swiss Alps and Scandinavian fiords. Explorers, scientists, and later painters and photographers, made Americans aware of these monumental landscapes. At the urging of Israel Ward Raymond, the San Francisco agent of Cornelius Vanderbilt's Central American Steamship Transit Company of New York, Union Republican California Senator John Conness introduced legislation to reserve Yosemite

George Catlin (1796–1872), ***Prairie Meadows Burning*** (1832). Oil on canvas, 11 x 14 1/8 (27.8 x 35.7 cm). Smithsonian American Art Museum, Washington, D.C. *Photo courtesy Art Resource/ N.Y.*

Valley and Mariposa Grove in the Sierra. Congress passed the bill and President Lincoln signed it on June 30, 1864. The park was administered by the State of California, but was poorly managed and minimally funded. Sheep herding and other destructive practices were rampant in the scenic valley.

At Yellowstone in Wyoming Territory, Congress reserved a much larger park of over 2 million acres. The National Park Service considers it the first national park. Containing half of the world's geothermal features and two-thirds of the world's geysers, it was obvious to many who first explored it that it should

be withdrawn from private purchase. The most consistent and effective voice for reservation was naturalist Ferdinand Vandeveer Hayden. In 1871, the government sponsored the Hayden Geological Survey, whose comprehensive report to Congress's Committee on Public Lands included large-format photographs by William Henry Jackson and paintings by Thomas Moran. On March 1, 1872, President Ulysses S. Grant signed the act that reserved Yellowstone "as a public park." Nathaniel P. Langford was appointed the first park superintendent but was denied a salary, funding, or staff. "Reservation was possible because most private interests were not looking so far west at this early date, for there were no railroads within hundreds of miles of Yellowstone."[2] When Yellowstone and the other early parks were reserved, neither the keystone predator role of aboriginal

Thomas Moran (1837-1926), ***The Grand Canyon of the Yellowstone*** (1893-1901). Oil on canvas, 96-1/2 x 168-3/8 in. (245.1 x 427.8 cm). Gift of George D. Pratt. Smithsonian American Art Museum, Washington, D.C. *Photo courtesy Art Resource/ N.Y.*

sending cavalry to Yosemite in the summers and building Camp Sheridan in Yellowstone in 1886. It was to be 30 years before Congress established any more national parks.

According to John Ise, one of the few historians to ponder the deep meaning of parks, "[T]he national park idea evolved to fill cultural rather than environmental needs. The search for a distinct national identity, more than what have come to be called 'the rights of rocks,' was the initial impetus behind scenic preservation. ... Thus the natural marvels of the West compensated for America's lack of old cities, aristocratic traditions, and similar reminders of Old World accomplishments. ... [The grand natural wonders of the unspoiled West] might now comfort people still living under the shadow of Milton, Shakespeare, and the Sistine Chapel."[3] The creation of national parks was part of the process of the creation of a national identity and the process of continental expansion westward. They were, at first, more national icons than places of recreation or of biological preservation. But as biological diversity began to shrink in the face of development, the parks were seen as sanctuaries for nature.

"Worthless" Lands, National Parks, and Rights of Way

In the 19th century, there was a national consensus that public lands were to be sold off as quickly as practicable and their resources exploited. Ranchers, farmers, timber companies, mine operators, and land speculators spoke through congressional delegations. Congress refused to reserve potentially productive lands. Even some Indian reservations were broken up for sale. Only "worthless"

hunting nor the importance of fire-setting by native peoples was understood. The aboriginal inhabitants were removed from the park and the surrounding area and confined on distant reservations. Without hunters, and with the provision of artificial feed in the winter, the population of elk exploded. By the 1930s, park managers had to cull or remove elk to protect the range lands. By default, the U.S. Army became the guardians of the early parks, lands, mostly rocky, snow-clad mountain peaks—but not the valuable forested foothills around them—were considered eligible for national parks. In 1901, Congress passed the Right of Way Act permitting rights of way through forest reserves and national parks for electrical, telegraph, and telephone lines, and irrigation and dam projects. Generally speaking, opposition to national parks was strongest in the Senate, where the lightly-populated West has always been over-represented. Support for parks was strongest in the populous East and in the more fairly apportioned House of Representatives.

Civil War Battlefields, 1890s

In the early 1890s, a generation after the Civil War, Congress began establishing national military parks: Chickamauga and Chattanooga National Military Park, and Antietam Battlefield, in 1890; Shiloh in 1894; and Gettysburg in 1895. More southern battlefields were added later. They were originally administered by the War Department but were transferred to the National Park Service in 1933 along with various other military and historical sites and 11 national cemeteries. Today, after marking the sesquicentennial of the Civil War, about 75 National Park Service sites memorialize the great rupture. Since the 1980s, interpretive programs at sites like Gettysburg have been updated to include the causes and consequences of the war. Post-war reconciliation and battlefield reunions are now explained within the larger context of African American disenfranchisement and segregation in the years following failed Reconstruction. Preserving both the land and the viewsheds of Civil War battlefields is now an issue as suburban and Big Box development spreads across the once-rural, fast-growing Southeast. The

55,000-member Civil War Trust founded in 1987 works to protect threatened battlefields by buying land to add to parks, accepting conservation easements, encouraging historical education, and engaging politically at the local and state level to thwart intrusive development.

Railroads, Enlightened Self-Interest, and Great Western Parks

Only one great economic interest backed the creation of national parks in the 19th century: the transcontinental railroads that passed them, especially the Northern Pacific Railroad that provided access to remote Yellowstone. The Northern Pacific invested in major destination hotels to provide attractive lodging in Yellowstone. In California, the powerful Southern Pacific Railroad supported the expansion of Yosemite. Later, the Great Northern Railroad built hotels in Glacier National Park (whose creation it promoted), and the Santa Fe Railroad built a destination hotel on the south rim of the Grand Canyon. The major railroads funded exhibits and publications on the national parks and featured them in their advertising. Stimulating national visitation, or dreams of visitation, helped create a national constituency for national parks. Many urban easterners became long-distance western park supporters.

Yosemite Expansion, 1890s

California did a poor job of protecting Yosemite Valley. The great advocate for Yosemite was geologist, writer, and mystic John Muir of California, who hiked much of the West Coast and parts of Alaska. Muir was a preservationist who sought to protect nature so that humans could, as he put it, commune with forces greater than themselves. With Robert Underwood Johnson, editor of the *Century* magazine

American bison in the Theodore Roosevelt National Park, North Dakota.

iStock photo by ericfoltz

in New York, Muir launched a campaign to expand Yosemite. In 1890, Congress established a much larger Yosemite National Park, and in 1906 California transferred the valley itself to the national park. Sequoia and General Grant (renamed Kings Canyon), two adjoining areas south of Yosemite, were also made national parks in 1890 to stop the wanton destruction of the giant sequoias, which were being dynamited into splinters to make shingles. Muir helped organize the Sierra Club in San Francisco in 1892 that brought together like-minded mountain hikers and later evolved into a strong national voice for parks and the environment.

Forest Reserves, Utilitarian Conservation, and the U.S. Forest Service, 1905

In 1891, responding to the demands of farmer-irrigators to preserve western watersheds, Congress repealed the Timber Culture Act of 1873 and several other laws, and passed the General Land Law Revision Act, also known as the Creative Act or the

Forest Reserve Act. It gave the president the power to set aside parts of the public domain as forest reservations without specific congressional authorization. It was only a few lines anonymously added to the land law revision in a congressional conference committee, but it turned out to be "the most important measure in the history of [U.S.] conservation".[4] The first reserve was the Yellowstone Forest Reserve. But Congress did not establish a means of managing these reserves until the Forest Management Act of 1897. Presidents Harrison, Cleveland, and McKinley quietly set aside a total of 27 million acres in the West. President Theodore Roosevelt seized the opportunity and added 148 million acres. TR, arguably the most influential conservationist in U.S. history, eventually placed more than 230 million acres under federal protection. These forest reserves are *not* national parks. They were, and remain, open to timber cutting, mining, land reclamation, grazing and oil leases, waterpower and irrigation development, and hunting and fishing, as well as passive recreation. In 1898, forester Gifford Pinchot became the first head of the Division of Forestry within the Department of Agriculture. Pinchot considered trees a crop and maneuvered to have the forest reserves transferred from the General Land Office in the Department of the Interior into his own Bureau of Forestry within the Department of Agriculture in 1905. Pinchot sought the efficient *use* of natural resources, not their unimpaired preservation. Pinchot claimed that "wilderness is waste." He later opposed the creation of national parks, many of which were carved out of "his" forest reserves. Today, these reserves are called *national forests* and serve as many visitors as the national parks do. Separately managed national forests surround many western national parks.

John F. Lacey and Southwestern Antiquities, Theodore Roosevelt and National Monuments, 1906

In 1902, Republican congressman John F. Lacey of Iowa visited northern New Mexico where archeologist-anthropologist Edgar Lee Hewett took him on a tour of the depredations of pot hunters in the ancient Indian ruins. Lacey had Hewett write a report to Congress describing the endangered archeological riches of the Southwest. In 1906, Lacey introduced, and Congress passed, the Act for the Preservation of American Antiquities to preserve "objects of historic or cultural interest that are situated upon lands owned or controlled by the Government of the United States." The intent of the Lacey Act was to preserve Indian cliff dwellings and other archeological sites in the Southwest. As in the creation of forest reserves, the act empowered the president to proclaim antiquities as *national monuments* without specific authorization by Congress and to withdraw such public land from sale. Oddly,

Theodore Roosevelt's first use of the act was not to preserve Indian antiquities but to establish Devil's Tower National Monument in Wyoming, a scenic or geological treasure, not a human antiquity. Over time, presidents proclaimed a great variety of national monuments, including natural sites from mountains to deserts and historical sites, from archeological ruins to battlefields to the homes of famous Americans.

In 1908, President Theodore Roosevelt used the Antiquities Act to set aside 800,000 acres in Arizona Territory for the Grand Canyon National Monument, stretching the act's intent considerably. By 1909, Roosevelt had proclaimed 18 national monuments. Many of them remained under the Forest Service, which administered them as multiple-use areas allowing grazing and lumbering. The distinction between national parks and national monuments has never been hard and fast except that parks are larger and monuments are usually smaller. Some large national monuments such as Grand Canyon were later made national parks.

Pro-Park Scientific, Conservation, and Civic Associations

From the mid-19th century to about 1920, many professional associations and natural history museums emerged from a variety of constituencies. Most were founded by educated, influential elites and were headquartered in major cities. They became respected lobbyists in Congress working for the creation of national parks and defended the parks from attempts to "open them up" to timber cutting, mining, and waterpower and irrigation projects. The first National Park Conference was held at Yellowstone, Wyoming, in September 1911. The independent and

Iowa Congressman John F. Lacey (1841-1913), author of the 1906 Act for the Preservation of American Antiquities, known as the Lacey Act.

staunchly preservationist National Parks Association, today the National Parks Conservation Association, was organized in Washington, D.C., in 1919.

American Geographical Society, New York, 1851

California Academy of Sciences, San Francisco, 1853

National Academy of Sciences, Washington, D.C., 1862

Peabody Museum of Archeology and Ethnology, Harvard, 1866

American Museum of Natural History, New York, 1869

White Mountain Club, 1873

American Forestry Association, Chicago, 1875

Rocky Mountain Club, Denver, 1875

Appalachian Mountain Club, Boston, 1876

Bureau of American Ethnology, Washington, D.C., 1879

American Association for the Advancement of Science, Philadelphia, 1880

American Ornithologists' Union, New York, 1883

Carnegie Museum of Natural History, Pittsburgh, 1885

National Audubon Society, New York, 1886

Boone and Crockett Club, New York and Washington, D.C., 1887

Geological Society of America, New York, 1888

National Geographic Society, Washington, D.C., 1888

Federation of Women's Clubs, New York, 1890

Sierra Club, San Francisco, 1892

Field Museum of Natural History, Chicago, 1893

New York Zoological Society, 1895, today the Wildlife Conservation Society

American Scenic and Historical Society, New York, 1895

Campfire Club of America, Chappaqua, N.Y., 1897

Society of American Foresters, Washington, D.C., 1900

Alpine Club, New York, 1902

American Civic Association, Washington, D.C., 1904

National Association of Audubon Societies, 1905

Seattle Mountaineers, 1906

National Conservation Association, Washington, D.C., 1909

Wildlife Protective Association, 1910

American Game Protective and Propagation Association, 1911

Hawaii Volcano Research Association, 1912

Permanent Wildlife Protection Fund, New York, 1913

Ecological Society of America, Washington, D.C., 1915

Save-the-Redwoods League, San Francisco, 1918

National Parks Association, Washington, D.C., 1919

Izaak Walton League, Gaithersburg, Md., 1922

Monumental Landscapes and New Parks

When Congress resumed designating national parks after a long pause, it focused on monumental landscapes, especially majestic mountains. Mount Rainier, Washington (1899); Crater Lake, Oregon (1902); Mesa Verde, Colorado, principally for its archeological ruins (1906); Glacier, Montana (1910); Rocky Mountain, Colorado (1915); Hawaii Volcanoes on the Big Island and Maui; and Lassen Volcanic, California (1916), were all made national parks and put under the secretary of the interior before there was a National Park Service to manage and protect them. None of these parks was created to preserve wildlife, nor were their boundaries drawn to embrace coherent ecosystems. Congress continued to make only random, token appropriations for the national parks into the early 20th century.

National Parks Under Attack

The mayor of San Francisco petitioned the secretary of the interior for permission to dam scenic Hetch Hetchy Valley in Yosemite National Park for the city's water supply in 1901. An epic battle between preservation and exploitation raged until 1913, when Congress and President Taft approved the dam and permitted the city to flood the magnificent valley. It was John Muir's and the Sierra Club's bitterest defeat. In 1907, the Colorado legislature and ranching and mining interests hosted

the Denver Public Lands Convention to advocate ceding the public domain to the states and restricting the setting aside of more national forests. The political-bureaucratic tide turned against national parks during the Woodrow Wilson administration. Forest Service and Reclamation Service engineers pushed back against "locking up" western timber and water in parks. In 1915, Olympic National Monument in Washington was cut in half to allow timber cutting in its ancient rainforest, and the proposed Rocky Mountain National Park was reduced by two-thirds before its creation in the same year.

Establishing the National Park Service, 1916

In 1900, Republican Representative John F. Lacey of Iowa introduced the first bill to properly administer national parks. It did not become law. In 1906 and 1907, Gifford Pinchot prepared bills for Congress to place the national parks under the Forest Service so that they could be opened up for natural resource development. His bureaucratic overreach backfired. Representative Lacey and others who advocated preservationist conservation, the keeping of natural areas in their original state, realized that parks needed their own bureaucracy within the government to counterbalance the "wise use" utilitarian conservationists in the Forest Service. They advocated the establishment of a separate federal agency within the Department of the Interior to manage national parks with a specifically preservationist mandate. (Canada had established its Dominion Parks Branch in 1911. Canada, Australia and New Zealand were the first countries to create national parks on the U.S. model.) Until 1916, each of the existing 14 national parks and 21 national monuments was administered separately under the

Stephen T. Mather (1867–1930), first director of the National Park Service.
Courtesy of the Library of Congress

overburdened secretary of the interior. There were no agreed-upon standards as to what was worthy of being a national park. Political pressure created small national parks at Wind Cave, South Dakota, Sullys Hill, North Dakota, Platt Park, Oklahoma and Mackinac Island, Michigan, none of which, in the opinion of critics, merited the distinction. In 1912, President Taft proposed the establishment of a Bureau of National Parks. Not until Progressive Republican/Independent Representative William Kent of California introduced a bill in 1916, probably drafted with the help of urban park designer Frederick Law Olmsted, Jr., did park administration get the attention of

Congress. Chicago businessman Stephen T. Mather, Horace McFarland of the American Civic Association, and publicist Robert Sterling Yard, among others, lobbied for the legislation. After passage in the House, Republican Senator Reed Smoot of Utah shepherded it through the Senate. In a compromise with western ranchers, the final bill authorized the secretary of the interior to permit grazing in the parks except at Yellowstone. President Wilson signed it into law on Aug. 25, 1916, creating the National Park Service within the Department of Interior. The Organic Act called for the parks to be managed so as to *"conserve the scenery and the natural and historic objects and the wild life therein and to provide for the enjoyment of the same in such a manner and by such means as will leave them unimpaired for the enjoyment of future generations."* Balancing resource protection with the needs of visitors has always been a fundamental issue in park management. Today, some scientists question whether parks can remain "unimpaired" in a world undergoing profound change due to human activity (anthropogenic change). The National Parks Association (today the National Parks Conservation Association) was founded in 1919 to advocate for the new park system.

The first National Park Service director was Californian Steven Mather, a borax mining millionaire, mountain climber, and indefatigable park promoter. He served from 1917 until his death in 1928 and set high standards for the new agency. Among his achievements was the creation of a cadre of professional National Park Rangers to manage, guard, and interpret the parks. Mather mobilized the General Federation of Women's Clubs to lobby Congress for the parks. He reached an

Montezuma Castle National Monument, Arizona.
iStock photo by luchsen

even larger public through the *National Geographic* and the *Saturday Evening Post,* vigorously advocating the preservationist philosophy to counter utilitarian conservationists. Director Maher spent his own money to hire pioneer publicist Robert Sterling Yard to promote the national parks. Mather's policies were continued by his like-minded successor, California lawyer Horace Albright. Public entertainment became part of the early effort to get the public to come to the remote parks. This included bear feeding shows, Indian rodeos, caged menageries, outdoor sports, and the summer fire-fall at Yosemite Valley. The Park Service later moved away from these popular spectacles.

From Scenery to Wildlife

The first national parks were created to protect scenic landscapes, not the wildlife that lived in them or that migrated in and out of them. Yellowstone was a prime example. There the large park protected high land, but the elk and other wildlife migrated to lower elevations during the winter to forage. As soon as they left the park boundary, they were fair game for hunters. A fundamental problem in most national parks is that their boundaries were not drawn with complete ecosystems in mind. In its early years, the National Park Service killed predators such as wolves, mountain lions, and coyotes. With no natural predators, elk, buffalo, moose, deer, and other wildlife proliferated, overgrazing the land. It was not until the mid-1930s that the "balance of nature"—the necessary relationship between predators and prey—was understood. In 1939, the National Park Service stopped eliminating native predators. In 1995, the Park Service reintroduced wolves to Yellowstone, an unpopular idea with ranchers.

Federal protection for wildlife began in 1903 when Frank Chapman, ornithologist at the American Museum of Natural History, persuaded Theodore Roosevelt to proclaim five-acre Pelican Island on Indian River, Florida, a refuge and breeding ground for native birds, especially egrets that were being slaughtered for ladies' hats. Roosevelt eventually established 53 wildlife sanctuaries separate from the national parks. Since 1940, wildlife refuges are managed by the U.S. Fish and Wildlife Service within the Department of the Interior. Everglades National Park, approved in 1934 and established in 1947, was the first park to be established as a "wilderness" to preserve wildlife, specifically subtropical birds.

Balancing West and East in the 1920s and '30s

The first great national parks were all in the remote Far West where there was abundant federal land and where population was sparse. In the eastern states the land had been privatized long ago, and Congress was opposed to buying private land for parks. National Park Service Directors Mather and Albright enlisted the support of the nation's financial, political, professional, and social elite for the parks. They knew that to gain national support for national parks they needed to add parks in the East. Proposals in Congress for the creation of a national park in western North Carolina and eastern Tennessee dated back to 1900, but lumber companies owned most of the land. State bond issues in North Carolina and Tennessee were crucial for land purchases, as was John D. Rockefeller, Jr.'s gift of $5 million in matching funds. (Rockefeller later quietly bought key lands to donate for Grand Teton, Acadia, Great Smoky Mountains and Virgin

Islands national parks. Today the John D. Rockefeller, Jr. Memorial Parkway links Grand Teton with Yellowstone.) Congress eventually appropriated some funds for land purchases for Great Smoky Mountains National Park. Congress often established parks that took many years to complete by accumulating properties from states or private owners. The Great Smoky Mountains National Park was established in 1926 but not dedicated until 1940. The second eastern national park was the smaller Shenandoah Park along the crest of the Blue Ridge Mountains in northern Virginia, with its 105-mile-long Skyline Drive. It was dedicated in 1936.

Herbert Hoover and New National Parks and Monuments

President Herbert Hoover had been president of the National Parks Association and supported the creation of several new national parks during his administration, including Grand Teton, Wyoming, Carlsbad Caverns, New Mexico, and Isle Royale, Michigan. Hoover also proclaimed national monuments at Badlands, South Dakota; Canyon de Chelly, Sunset Crater and Saguaro, Arizona; Great Sand Dunes, Colorado; White Sands, New Mexico; Grand Canyon and Black Canyon, Colorado, and Death Valley, California.

Franklin D. Roosevelt and National Monuments and Historic Sites

President Franklin D. Roosevelt, like his distant cousin Theodore Roosevelt, was an ardent conservationist and park advocate. In 1933, a Democratic Congress gave FDR the power to reorganize federal executive and administrative agencies. Roosevelt appointed Harold L. Ickes, a staunch park advocate, to be secretary of the interior, and Arno B. Cammerer became director of the National Park Service. At the urging of Horace Albright, all national military

parks, as well as battlefield sites, national historical monuments and national cemeteries under the War Department, were transferred to the Department of the Interior's National Park Service. National monuments on U.S. Forest Service lands were also transferred to the National Park Service. The NPS became responsible for all federal parks and monuments in Washington, D.C. The result was that the NPS now managed sites as varied as the National Mall, the Washington Monument, the President's Garden (White House grounds), the Statue of Liberty, and Independence Hall. Over 100 historical buildings and areas became units of the National Park Service, many of them in the populous East, making the park system truly national. It now embraced much more than just scenic parks in the remote Far West. This broadened the base of political support for what was now a truly *national* system of parks.

Theodore Roosevelt and John Muir on Glacier Point, Yosemite Valley, California, in 1903.
Courtesy of the Library of Congress

Other innovative New Deal policies included the Historic Sites and Building Acts of 1935 that first called for surveys of historic and archeological sites and led to the establishment of the National Register of Historic Places, managed by the NPS. After 1936, eminent historians, archeologists, and architects served on the Advisory Board on National Parks, Historic Sites, Buildings and Monuments and helped guide federal policies. New Deal employment projects including the Civilian Conservation Corps, the Public Works Administration, and the Works Projects Administration put the unemployed to work on soil and forest conservation projects and building roads, trails, and lodges in national parks. A five-year Parks, Parkway and Recreation Area Study assessed national recreation needs. Recreation Areas were constructed near major cities and at federal reservoirs, including Lake Mead, Nevada/Arizona, and those of the Tennessee Valley Authority. The federal government had never been so proactive in parks and recreation. Finally, several national parkways begun as public works employment projects were also put under the NPS, including the Blue Ridge Parkway, North Carolina and Virginia, the Natchez Trace Parkway, Tennessee and Mississippi, and parkways around Washington, D.C. Cape Hatteras, North Carolina, became the first national seashore, another New Deal innovation. It took about 30 years for the National Park Service to assimilate all these new responsibilities.

During World War II, the National Park Service office relocated to Chicago, and park funding fell from $21.1 million in 1940 to $4.6 million in 1944. There were also wartime demands to open the parks to timber cutting, mining, and grazing. In 1951, NPS Director Newton B. Drury resigned in

protest over Bureau of Reclamation plans to dam Dinosaur National Monument, Utah.

Automobiles, Development, and the Call for Wilderness

In the 1920s and '30s, automobiles began to replace railroads as the principal means of access to the parks. This shifted park visitation from principally the upper class to include the middle class as well. (The poor have never had equal access to the distant great national parks in the West.) The issue of visitor services in the parks, especially overnight accommodations, was a constant challenge in the parks, because leases were short (usually 10 years) and financial returns were often insufficient, as many parks are only busy in the summer. More roads and facilities in parks stimulated preservationists to call for roadless, or wilderness, areas. The Wilderness Society organized in Washington, D.C., in 1935. Cape Hatteras National Seashore, North Carolina, established in 1937, was the first park specifically established "as a primitive wilderness." With the end of war-time gasoline rationing and the spread of the automobile, park visitation boomed from 6 million in 1942 to 33 million in 1950. Summer road trips to the great national parks in the West became a tradition for many middle-class American families. To cope with increased visitation, the Park Service undertook a $1 billion program of new roads, campgrounds, trails, and visitor centers from 1956 to 1966 dubbed Mission 66. Controversy over some Mission 66 projects helped spur the passage of the Wilderness Act of 1964.

Science Enters the Parks

In 1864, Vermonter George Perkins Marsh published *Man and Nature; or, Physical Geography as Modified by Human*

Action, the first analysis of humanity's destructive impact on the environment, what we now call anthropogenic change. In 1866, German biologist Ernst Haeckel coined the word "ecology." It took about 100 years for public opinion to absorb these concepts. The National Park Service itself was slow to accept the need for science-based park management. One of the first to do so was George Melendez Wright, an assistant park naturalist at Yosemite, who began a wildlife survey in 1929, which he himself funded. In 1930, he became the first chief of the wildlife division of the National Park Service, and each park began to survey its wildlife and identify problems. Wright recognized that parks were not biological islands and that natural and cultural resources had to be managed as one. In 1963, Department of the Interior Secretary Stewart Udall commissioned wildlife biologist A. Starker Leopold of the University of California to rethink wildlife management in the parks. In that same year, a committee of the National Academy of Sciences chaired by William Robbins produced a plan calling for scientific research in the parks in order to guide their management. These two studies eventually led to new ways of thinking about natural resources management. The gist of these two reports was the (now contested) idea that nature seeks equilibrium and that "natural" processes lead to "natural" results and that thus it is possible to perpetuate park resources "unimpaired" as the Organic Act of 1916 legislated.

The Ecological and Environmental Revolution of the 1960s and '70s

How Americans understood their environment changed profoundly between the mid-1960s and the mid-1970s. Unprecedented landmark legislation set the country on a new path intended to

protect natural and cultural resources and to balance conservation and development. In 1964, over the resistance of the National Park Service, Congress passed the National Wilderness Preservation System Act to protect areas of 5,000 acres (2,023 hectares) or larger "retaining its primeval character and influence, without permanent improvements or human habitation, which is protected and managed so as to preserve its natural conditions...." These wilderness areas became the most protected federal lands in the U.S. In 1966, the National Historic Preservation Act gave protection to historic buildings, and Section 4(f) of the Department of Transportation Act prohibited spending federal funds on the construction of roads through parkland if a feasible alternative was available. The Air Quality Act of 1967 mandated control of air pollution. The Wild and Scenic Rivers Act passed in 1968. A

A. Starker Leopold, author of the 1963 Leopold Report on wildlife and ecosystem management in U.S. national parks, a seminal work in the conservation movement.
Photo copyright the Aldo Leopold Foundation

major underwater oil well blow-out off the coast of Santa Barbara, California, in 1969 focused media attention on the fragile environment. In 1969, Congress passed the National Environmental Policy Act (NEPA) requiring environmental impact reports for all projects with federal funding. NEPA also mandated public participation and empowered citizens to challenge agency decisions. In 1972, the Clean Water Act curbed water pollution. In 1973, the Endangered Species Act extended protection to plants and animals on the verge of extinction. (Though the act requires that all endangered species be recovered, there are no provisions that help managers in prioritizing one species' survival over another.) In 1974, the Archeological and Historic Preservation Act was passed. In 1976, Historic Preservation Tax Incentives managed by the NPS and the IRS began channeling private investment toward income-producing historic buildings. By 2006, tax incentives had leveraged over $33 billion to rehabilitate historic properties. In 1978, Congress passed the National Parks and Recreation Act that required each park to prepare a General Management Plan. The act also authorized a $1.2 billion program for urban and national parks. The modern park plans that emerged placed more emphasis on ecosystem preservation than on tourism.

New Environmental Organizations Emerge, but Not a National Green Party

In the 1960s and 1970s, a new wave of nonprofit, non-partisan, member-supported environmental and conservation advocacy organizations emerged as the environmental movement gathered strength. The Sierra Club, founded in 1892 in San Francisco by mountain hikers, evolved into a general environmental organization with a national scope. Wikipedia listed 108 environmental organizations in the U.S. in 2012. They range from the Abalone Alliance to Earth First!, the Green Zionist Alliance, Public Employees for Environmental Responsibility to the Ocean Conservancy. Some organizations have a local focus, others national, and still others global missions. While it is difficult to make generalizations about these varied organizations, it is safe to say that their cumulative impact is significant. They allow citizens to participate at many levels, from financial donations and legacies to volunteering opportunities, political mobilization, and the satisfaction of being a part of something greater than themselves of national and enduring importance.

What is distinctive about the U.S., as opposed to Western Europe and some other nations, is that there is no strong Green Party in the United States that consistently appears on national ballots. Unlike Western Europe where Green Parties, though small, can have influence in coalition governments, most U.S. environmental organizations work to pressure Congress on pending legislation and monitor the federal departments responsible for public lands administration and the enforcement of environmental laws. Lawsuits in federal courts are often environmentalist organizations' most effective tool in stopping destructive projects or policies.

Nonprofit status under the Internal Revenue Service prevents environmental organizations from actively engaging in partisan political campaigns, even though environmental protection is fundamentally a political issue.

The Creation of the Land and Water Conservation Fund, 1965

In 1965, the Land and Water Conservation Fund was established with 90 percent of the monies from offshore oil and gas leases on the federally owned outer continental shelf. Each administration proposes, and then Congress must appropriate, expenditures annually. The fund permits federal agencies, including the National Park Service, to buy land. The NPS uses these appropriations to purchase inholdings, to expand park boundaries, and to create national lakeshores, wild and scenic rivers, and national trails. The fund also makes 50 percent matching grants to states for state and local parks, including new playgrounds, baseball diamonds, and soccer fields. The fund is authorized at $900 million annually, but that level has only been met twice in 40 years. From 1965 to 2006, about $29 billion was credited to the fund, but only half that amount, $14.3 billion, was appropriated to federal, state, and local projects. Federal land acquisition accounted for 62 percent, state grants 28 percent, and other programs 10 percent of the $14.3 billion. Prohibitions on the use of the fund for maintenance (a critical national park need), for conservation easements, or for managing ecosystems that include both federal and private land, limit the usefulness of the Land and Water Conservation Fund.

National Scenic and Historic Trails

The first section of the 2,175-mile long Appalachian Trail was blazed in 1923. It could be walked end-to-end by 1938. Today it traverses 14 eastern states. The National Trails System Act of 1968 allowed the establishment of a network of scenic, historic, and recreational trails for hiking and riding. Most were established

in the late 1970s, 1980s, and 1990s. A distinctive feature of the national trails is their reliance on independent, volunteer-based, partner organizations. Most trails also involve interagency collaborations among two or three federal agencies. Of today's 29 trails, 17 are managed by the National Park Service, and the others by the U.S. Forest Service or the Bureau of Land Management. Most national trails have no boundaries and no on-site staff. The most recent is the 54-mile long (87 kilometers) Selma to Montgomery National Historic Trail in Alabama, commemorating the marches of civil rights activists in the spring of 1965 that spurred the passage of the Voting Rights Act.

Wild and Scenic Rivers

Congress passed the Wild and Scenic Rivers Act in 1968. Rivers, or sections of rivers so designated, are preserved in their free-flowing condition and may not be dammed or otherwise impeded. The rivers that flow through federal lands are managed by one or more federal agencies including the National Park Service. Designation as a wild and scenic river is not the same as national park designation. Wild and Scenic Partnership Rivers are those that flow through private lands and lands owned by state and local governments. As of 2009, there were 252 designated wild and scenic rivers.

National Marine Sanctuaries and NOAA

In the wake of the 1969 Santa Barbara underwater oil well blow-out in California, Congress passed the Marine Protection, Research and Sanctuaries Act in 1972. Today 14 National Marine Sanctuaries protect some 150,000 square miles and are administered by the National Oceanic and Atmospheric Administration (NOAA).

Few Americans other than fishermen are aware of these underwater "national parks." They are especially important as havens where fish can breed undisturbed and replenish their populations.

Richard Nixon Brings "Parks to the People"

President Nixon's Secretary of the Interior, former Alaska Governor Walter Hickel, was a maverick combination of real estate developer, utilitarian conservationist, and environmentalist. He embraced existing planning for new national parks close to major cities through the conversion of minimally used historic military reservations into parks. Under far-seeing National Parks Service Director George B. Hartzog, Jr., the park system opened its upper ranks to women and African Americans. Hartzog added 69 areas to the system, including two major parks of a new kind: Gateway National Recreation Area in New Jersey and New York framing the entrance to New York Harbor, and the Golden Gate National Recreation Area in the San Francisco Bay Area. Both consisted principally of former Army harbor defense reservations. These parks, established in 1972, forced a change in National Park Service thinking from preserving remote wild places to also converting and restoring altered landscapes adjacent to urban areas accessible to city dwellers. Since their creation, these parks have worked to attract underserved urban communities, especially minority youth. (President Nixon forced Hartzog to resign when the NPS revoked a special use permit that allowed Nixon's crony, Bebe Rebozo, to dock his houseboat at Biscayne National Monument, Florida.)

Jimmy Carter and the Great Alaskan Parks Expansion

The United States purchased Alaska from Russia in 1867. It remained a territory until statehood in 1959. Alaska contains the largest federally owned public domain in the U.S., including vast tracts of wilderness. The discovery of oil at Prudhoe Bay in 1968 created pressure to resolve the issue of Native land claims in order to build the Trans-Alaska Pipeline. In 1971, President Nixon signed the Alaska Native Claims Settlement Act that confirmed Native ownership of 44 million acres, made a payment of $962 million to Native corporations, and directed the secretary of the interior to withdraw 80 million acres for potential designation as national parks, wildlife refuges, wild and scenic rivers, or national forests. In 1978, President Carter designated 56 million acres as national monuments, and the secretary of the interior withdrew an additional 40 million acres. This pressured Congress to resolve the impasse between preservationists and developers and pass the Alaska National Interest Lands Conservation Act in 1980. That act created 10 new national parks and expanded three existing parks for a total of 43.6 million acres, reserved 53.7 million acres for the National Wildlife Refuge system, set aside parts of 25 rivers as National Wild and Scenic Rivers, and designated 3.3 million acres as National Forest lands. This doubled the amount of land in the national parks and wildlife refuge systems and tripled the amount of land designated as wilderness. National Parks alone went from 31 million acres to 78 million acres. Today Alaska contains two-thirds of all national parklands. In a compromise with hunters, many Alaska parks are *national parks and preserves.* The "preserve" designation

Sunburst anemone, *Anthopleura sola*, and black turban snails, *Tegula funebralis*, in a tide pool. Monterey Bay National Marine Sanctuary, Monterey Bay, California.

iStock photo by NNehring

means that Native traditional subsistence activities such as trapping, hunting, and plant gathering are permitted, as well as regulated sport hunting.

Ronald Reagan and Secretary of the Interior James Watt

Ronald Reagan was sympathetic to the "Sagebrush Rebellion" in the western states that sought to open *all* federal lands to commercial and industrial uses. His appointment of James Watt of Wyoming as secretary of the interior in 1980 led to one of the most controversial periods in the Department of the Interior's history. Watt had been the secretary to the natural resources committee and environmental pollution advisory panel of the U.S. Chamber of Commerce and founded the libertarian Mountain States Legal Foundation that advocated expanded timber cutting, ranching, mining, and oil and gas drilling on federal lands. Watt was openly hostile to environmentalism, listing

species under the Endangered Species Act, or accepting donations of private land for conservation purposes. He sought to redirect funds from the Land and Water Conservation Fund used to expand wildlife refuges and national parks to park repairs, something it was not intended to cover. He restructured the Department of the Interior to decrease federal regulatory power and weaken mining regulations. The area leased to coal mining quintupled during his term as secretary. Watt favored opening wilderness areas and shore lands to oil and gas drilling. Funding and staffing did not keep up with the needs of national parks. Budget cuts contributed to an estimated $1.9 billion backlog in national park infrastructure improvements and repairs by 1988. Morale in the National Park Service plummeted under Secretary Watt. Watt was forced to resign in 1983 after reports of his derogatory remarks about the racial, religious, and gender composition of a Senate advisory panel.

Bill Clinton, the National Wildlife Refuge Improvement Act of 1997, and the First Call for Biodiversity Conservation

Congress passed, and President Clinton signed, a path-breaking "organic act" for the National Wildlife Refuge System in 1997. It gave the 540 refuges and other units, plus 37 wetland management districts, an overarching mission and mandated the implementation of an ecosystem-based approach to wildlife conservation by the United States Fish and Wildlife Service in the Department of the Interior. This was the first time that federal legislation required that "the biological diversity, integrity, and environmental health of the [refuge] system are maintained for the benefit of present and future generations of Americans." The refuges and other protected areas embrace 95 million acres of pristine land and waters, more than are in all the national parks. Once managed as separate islands, refuges are now envisioned as "hubs" adjacent to private, state, and federal lands mandated to promote conservation strategies beyond their boundaries and extending into the surrounding landscapes. Once focused primarily on waterfowl, refuges now conserve and protect all species and their habitats. The new law incorporates biodiversity conservation to a far greater extent than any other previous statute. The act includes a hierarchy of priorities to help managers rank competing goals.

George W. Bush versus the National Park Service: Utilitarian and Preservationist Conservationists Clash Again

After the pro-park preservationist policies of Bill Clinton, the tension between preservation and use in the national parks erupted anew under George W. Bush when he selected Gale Norton, a protégé of James Watt, to be secretary of the Department of the Interior. In 2003, the administration floated the idea of outsourcing up to 70 percent of all full-time jobs in the National Park Service, including those of natural resource experts, archeologists, biologists, historians, and museum curators. "Competitive sourcing" was also proposed for the Forest Service, the Fish and Wildlife Service, and the Bureau of Land Management. Preservationists and some park professionals saw this as a crippling of federal land management agencies so that private interests could enter the parks and exploit them. Park Service morale plummeted. The House committee overseeing the Interior Department balked at the outsourcing proposal.

Interior Deputy Assistant Secretary Paul Hoffman, the former head of the Cody, Wyoming Chamber of Commerce, drafted a revision of the *NPS Management Policies* in 2005. The draft deleted the language in the 1916 Organic Act stating that the mission of the NPS is to "conserve the scenery and that natural and historic objects and wildlife therein . . . in such a manner and by such means as will leave them unimpaired for future generations." It also replaced the words "preserve" and "protect" with "conserve," which to commercial interests implies so-called "wise use." The draft weakened land conservation policies, opened the parks to cell phone towers, allowed all-terrain vehicles, snowmobiles, personal water craft, and airplanes in wilderness areas, and permitted the sale of anti-scientific "creationist" books in park shops. These proposals sparked an outcry among NPS employees and environmental organizations. In 2006, NPS Director Fran Mainella rescinded the controversial draft.

In 2006, George W. Bush proclaimed the Papāhanaumokuākea Marine National Monument (the northwestern Hawaiian Islands) administered by NOAA, the U.S. Fish and Wildlife Service, and the State of Hawaii. It protects 139,797 square miles and some 7,000 marine species and is larger than all U.S. National Parks combined. In 2009, Bush proclaimed three marine protected areas in the Pacific, including the Mariana Islands, Palmyra Atoll, and Rose Atoll totaling more than 193,050 square miles.

Historical Sites Reflect a More Inclusive View of the American People

Two-thirds of National Park Service properties are historical sites, not nature reserves. They traditionally focused on places associated with the American Revolution, Civil War battlefields, and the homes of noted Americans, principally presidents and a few artists. Changes in immigration laws in 1965 under Lyndon Johnson led to dramatically increased diversity in the already diverse American population. At the same time, changes in academic and popular history focused attention on previously marginalized people, including women, Native Americans, African Americans, Latinos, and Asian Americans. This attention to social diversity has resulted in the creation of new parks and monuments and the reinterpretation of old ones. Native American-associated sites now include the Trail of Tears National Historic Trail, Georgia to Oklahoma; the Sand Creek Massacre National Historic Site, Colo.; and the Washita Battlefield National Historic Site, Okla., where the U.S.

Army attacked a Cheyenne village. The Custer Battlefield National Monument in Montana was renamed the Little Bighorn National Monument to include the Lakota, Cheyenne, and Arapaho as well as the U.S. Cavalry. These sites of conscience memorialize the tragic aspects of American expansion.

In the mid-1980s, NPS Director William Penn Mott, Jr. instructed the Park Service to include the role of slavery where appropriate in national parks. Today African Americans are memorialized at the African American Burial Ground National Monument, New York; Cane River Creole National Historical Park, Louisiana; Frederick Douglass National Historic Site in Washington, D.C.; George Washington Carver National Monument, Missouri; Booker T. Washington National Monument, Virginia; the Tuskegee Institute and Tuskegee Airmen National Historic Sites, Alabama; Boston African American National Historical Site, Massachusetts; Port Chicago Naval Magazine National Memorial, California; Brown v. Board of Education National Historic Site, Topeka, Kansas; Little Rock Central High School National Historic Site, Arkansas; Selma to Montgomery National Historic Trail, Alabama; and the Martin Luther King, Jr., National Historic Site, Atlanta, Georgia; and other sites.

The National Park Service initially focused on Spanish exploration and missions in Florida, the Southwest, and California rather than the long-enduring Latino settlements of the region. Many key sites such as the Palace of the Governors of 1610 in Santa Fe, the 21 California Franciscan missions, and the Alamo in San Antonio, shrine of the Texas Revolution of 1836, are state or privately managed sites, not federal properties. Early federal sites

Expanding Visions of the Park Service

In 1916, Congress established the National Park Service to conserve the parks and the "scenery and the natural and historic objects and the wildlife therein, unimpaired for the enjoyment of future generations." That legislative mandate was but the first of many expanding the Park Service mission to manage other natural, historic, and cultural resources beyond the boundaries of the 35 parks and monuments then existing. Among the milestones in the agency's journey to the present were the Preservation of Historic Sites Act of 1935, which shifted stewardship of national battle-fields from the Department of the Army to the Park Service, and the Alaska National Interest Lands Conservation Act of 1980, which increased the size of the National Park System from 31 million acres to 78 million. In between, the Park Service inherited such additional duties as administering the Land and Water Conservation Fund, wild and scenic rivers, national trails, and the National Register of Historic Places.

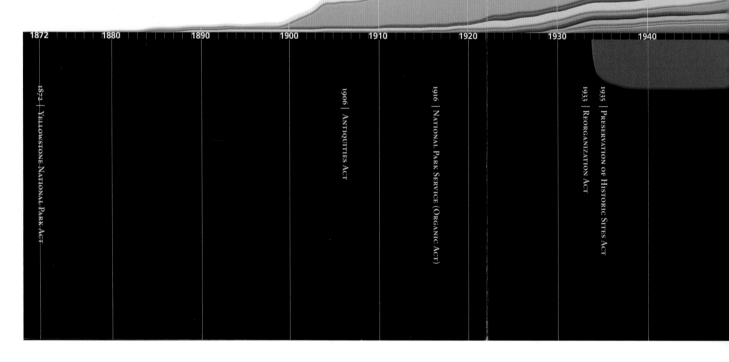

1872 | 1880 | 1890 | 1900 | 1910 | 1920 | 1930 | 1940

1872 | Yellowstone National Park Act

1906 | Antiquities Act

1916 | National Park Service (Organic Act)

1933 | Reorganization Act

1935 | Preservation of Historic Sites Act

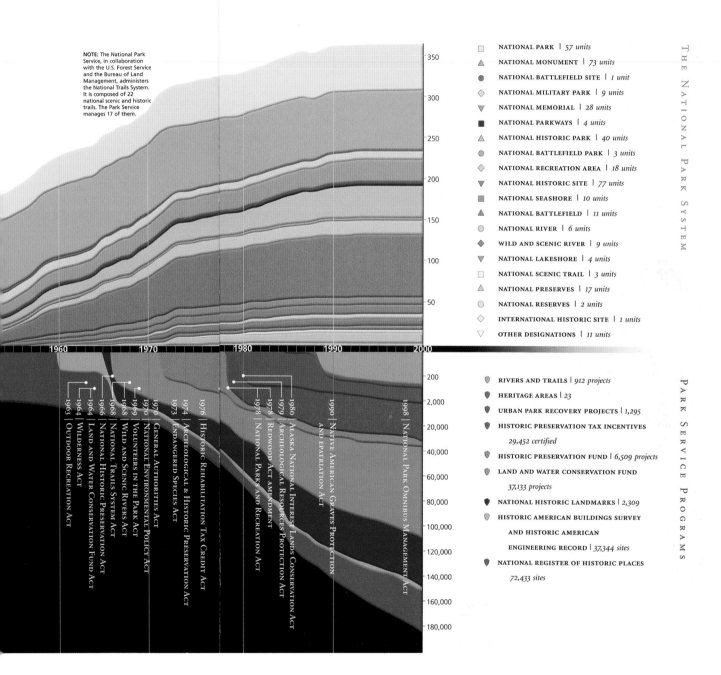

NOTE: The National Park Service, in collaboration with the U.S. Forest Service and the Bureau of Land Management, administers the National Trails System. It is composed of 22 national scenic and historic trails. The Park Service manages 17 of them.

□	NATIONAL PARK	57 units
△	NATIONAL MONUMENT	73 units
●	NATIONAL BATTLEFIELD SITE	1 unit
◇	NATIONAL MILITARY PARK	9 units
▽	NATIONAL MEMORIAL	28 units
■	NATIONAL PARKWAYS	4 units
△	NATIONAL HISTORIC PARK	40 units
◉	NATIONAL BATTLEFIELD PARK	3 units
◇	NATIONAL RECREATION AREA	18 units
▽	NATIONAL HISTORIC SITE	77 units
▦	NATIONAL SEASHORE	10 units
▲	NATIONAL BATTLEFIELD	11 units
○	NATIONAL RIVER	6 units
◆	WILD AND SCENIC RIVER	9 units
▽	NATIONAL LAKESHORE	4 units
□	NATIONAL SCENIC TRAIL	3 units
△	NATIONAL PRESERVE	17 units
◎	NATIONAL RESERVES	2 units
◇	INTERNATIONAL HISTORIC SITE	1 units
▽	OTHER DESIGNATIONS	11 units

	RIVERS AND TRAILS	912 projects
	HERITAGE AREAS	23
	URBAN PARK RECOVERY PROJECTS	1,295
	HISTORIC PRESERVATION TAX INCENTIVES	
	29,452 certified	
	HISTORIC PRESERVATION FUND	6,509 projects
	LAND AND WATER CONSERVATION FUND	
	37,133 projects	
	NATIONAL HISTORIC LANDMARKS	2,309
	HISTORIC AMERICAN BUILDINGS SURVEY	
	AND HISTORIC AMERICAN	
	ENGINEERING RECORD	37,344 sites
	NATIONAL REGISTER OF HISTORIC PLACES	
	72,433 sites	

Timeline acts:

1963 | OUTDOOR RECREATION ACT
1964 | WILDERNESS ACT
1964 | LAND AND WATER CONSERVATION FUND ACT
1966 | NATIONAL HISTORIC PRESERVATION ACT
1968 | NATIONAL TRAILS SYSTEM ACT
1968 | WILD AND SCENIC RIVERS ACT
1969 | VOLUNTEERS IN THE PARK ACT
1970 | NATIONAL ENVIRONMENTAL POLICY ACT
1970 | GENERAL AUTHORITIES ACT
1973 | ENDANGERED SPECIES ACT
1974 | ARCHEOLOGICAL & HISTORIC PRESERVATION ACT
1976 | HISTORIC REHABILITATION TAX CREDIT ACT
1978 | NATIONAL PARKS AND RECREATION ACT
1978 | REDWOOD ACT AMENDMENT
1979 | ARCHEOLOGICAL RESOURCES PROTECTION ACT
1980 | ALASKA NATIONAL INTEREST LANDS CONSERVATION ACT
1990 | NATIVE AMERICAN GRAVES PROTECTION AND REPATRIATION ACT
1998 | NATIONAL PARK OMNIBUS MANAGEMENT ACT

Growth of the National Park System and of Park Service Programs

Rethinking the National Parks for the 21st Century
National Park System Advisory Board Report, 2001

A **bighorn sheep,** Arches National Park, Utah.
Photo courtesy National Park Service

include El Morro National Monument, New Mexico, with its explorers' inscriptions, proclaimed in 1906; Tumacacori National Historical Park, Arizona, of 1908; and the Salinas Pueblo Missions National Monument, New Mexico, with its three 17th-century mission church sites and pueblo ruins, proclaimed in 1909. Cabrillo National Monument, California, Coronado National Memorial, Arizona, and De Soto National Monument, Florida, continued the theme of early Spanish exploration. The San Antonio Missions National Historical Park, Tex., continued the story of missions in the Spanish Southwest. The Castillo de San Marcos National Monument guarded Spanish St. Augustine, Florida, founded in 1565 and the oldest colonial city in the U.S. Here the Spanish and English empires clashed before there was a United States of America. The Salt River Bay National

Historical Park & Ecological Preserve, Virgin Islands, where Columbus clashed with the Caribs in 1493, and the massive Spanish fortifications at the San Juan National Historic Site, Puerto Rico, are key Caribbean sites. The Palo Alto National Battlefield and the Resaca de la Palma Battlefield, Texas, mark the taking by the U.S. of half of Mexico's territory and about 1 percent of her population in the Mexican-American War of 1846–48. The Mexican Cession encapsulated long-established Latino populations within the expanded United States, where they survived with little national attention. Not until the recent establishment of the four National Historic Trails between Texas and California was the theme of Latino *settlement* included: Camino Real de Tierra Adentro, New Mexico; Camino Real de los Tejas, Texas and Louisiana; the

Old Spanish Trail, New Mexico, Colorado, Utah, Nevada, and California; and the Anza Trail, Arizona to California. But the Latino settlement of the Southwest beginning with Hispano Santa Fe, New Mexico, in 1607–08, and then the recent migrations northward, indeed as far north as Chicago and Boston, remain to be recognized in their full national significance. In 2011, the National Park Service initiated the American Latino Heritage Initiative to more accurately present the Latino dimension of U.S. history.

The Lowell National Historical Park in Massachusetts, in partnership with the University of Massachusetts-Lowell, tells the story of industrialization, "mill girls," and the immigrants who worked in textile mills. Women's Rights National Historical Park, Seneca Falls, New York, commemorates the first women's rights convention in 1848. Rosie the Riveter/ World War II Home Front National Historical Park, California, honors women's work in the "arsenal of democracy." The First Ladies National Historical Site, Ohio, in the home of William and Ida Saxton McKinley, honors presidents' wives.

Recent sites of conscience are the Manzanar National Historic Site, California, and the Minidoka National Historic Site, Idaho, recalling the internment of innocent Japanese and Japanese-Americans in camps during World War II. The Kalaupapa National Historical Park, Hawaii, commemorates the forced quarantine of Hawaiians with Hansen's disease (leprosy) on the island of Molokai.
The legacy of modern warfare is also entering the national park system. In 1999, the Minuteman Missile National Historical Site opened in rural South Dakota, preserving an underground silo that once

held a solid-fuel Intercontinental Ballistic Missile and a nearby launch control facility, sobering reminders of nuclear warfare and the distinct possibility of "mutually assured destruction." The Flight 93 National Memorial in southwestern Pennsylvania remembers the 9/11 terrorist attacks in 2001.

National Heritage Areas

National Heritage Areas were inaugurated in 1984 and are separately established by Congress to encourage the historic preservation of nationally significant and unique natural, cultural, historic, and scenic places. There are 49 National Heritage Areas, ranging from factory towns and city neighborhoods to farmland and battlefields. They are not National Park Service units nor are they federally owned. They are administered by state governments, nonprofit organizations, or private corporations. The National Park Service advises them and provides limited technical, planning, and financial assistance. Some are known as National Heritage Corridors.

Affiliated Areas

Affiliated Areas were inaugurated in 1970 and comprise various significant, distinctive regional landscapes outside the National Park System. Some of these places have been recognized by acts of Congress and others by the secretary of the interior under the Historic Sites Act of 1935. These are places where people still live and work. There are 24 affiliated areas. Some are canal corridors, and others tell the story of steel, coal, or American agriculture. The National Parks Service provides technical and limited financial assistance to local partnership organizations in these affiliated areas.

Citizens' Advisory Commissions and Their Demise

Though national parks are just that, *national* entities, they are, of course, situated in particular locations and surrounded by local communities that naturally have a special relationship with "their" park. In the mid-1970s, when the idea of citizen participation was at its height and the National Park Service was launching its new initiative of bringing "parks to the people where the people are," a few new federal parks experimented with citizens' advisory commissions. Among the most noteworthy was the Citizens' Advisory Commission (CAC) for the Point Reyes National Seashore and the Golden Gate National Recreation Area (GGNRA) in northern California. The legislation for the GGNRA authorized an advisory commission. The secretary of the interior appointed 15 unpaid citizens for three-year terms. Six members were chosen by the secretary; the others were nominated by counties, regional government agencies, and local park activists. Although park superintendents retained sole responsibility for insuring that local park policies conformed to National Park Service policies, the CAC served as a conduit for citizen input, and conversely, as a way for park administrators to float proposals and gage public responses. The CAC helped generate local support for the parks and also helped minimize the antagonism of local agencies and organizations. But after 29 years, Congress, advised by the Park Service, did not reauthorize the Citizens' Advisory Commission, and it disbanded in 2002.

Nonprofit Cooperating Associations and National Parks

Federal appropriations have failed to keep up with national park and park programs expansion. One response has been the creation of locally based cooperating associations approved by the National Park Service but independently organized as nonprofit organizations. Most of these cooperating associations produce books and brochures and sell souvenirs in national park visitor centers. The more active associations also engage volunteers in their parks to care for habitat, wildlife, and trails, and also to raise funds from the local community and philanthropists. Volunteers, under Park Service expert supervision, weed out exotic plants and plant native species. Cooperating associations also provide educational and cultural classes, programs, and activities for schools and the general public supplementing, but not replacing, the work of park rangers. By 2012, of the 397 national park units, 158 have "friends groups" that help raise private funds. The congressionally chartered National Park Foundation is working to increase their number to 200 by 2016. Cooperating associations help root a park in its community, create a sense of ownership of national parks, and build political support for them. While cooperating associations are creative and important, they often work best in already wealthy regions, not in less fortunate parts of the nation. Thus they provide only a fraction of the system's $2.6 billion annual budget.

The most active and successful of these cooperating associations is the Golden Gate National Parks Conservancy, which supports the Golden Gate National Recreation Area in the San Francisco Bay Area. Organized in 1981, the conservancy has its offices in the GGNRA's headquarters building at Fort Mason in San Francisco. With its own well-connected board of directors and staff, it has successfully raised over $200 million to support an array of park

Great Blue Heron rookery,
Arches National Park, Utah.

NPS photo by Andrew Kuhn

projects and programs throughout the GGNRA, including the transformation of Crissy Army Airfield in the Presidio from 100 acres of pavement and hard-packed dirt into a recreated marsh, historic grass airfield, and popular bayside promenade. The conservancy also funds the Crissy Field Center, an environmental education center with outreach to underserved urban youth; the Trails Forever initiative, which builds new trails and overlooks throughout the GGNRA; and the Fort Baker Institute, an environmental think tank located at historic Fort Baker.

Land Trusts and Easements

Land trusts, also known as land conservancies, have existed in the U.S. since 1891 but have only become important in the last two decades at the same time that public funding for national and other parks began to plateau or decline. By 2012, there were 1,723 active land trusts in the nation operating in every one of the 50 states. The greatest numbers are in California, Massachusetts, Connecticut, and Pennsylvania, with the fastest growth in California, Nevada, and Hawaii. Land trusts are private, nonprofit organizations that actively work to conserve land by accepting conservation easements, acquiring land, accepting donations of land, or managing land easements. Land trusts exist to preserve sensitive natural areas with endangered plants or wildlife, farmland, ranchland, forests, deserts, water sources, or cultural landmarks such as archeological sites or battlefields. They operate at local levels as well as the international level through organizations such as the World Land

Trust. Conservation trusts often target lands adjacent to or inside existing parks or protected areas. Some land trusts hold land before public agencies can come up with the appropriated funds to buy them. Land trusts also sell to private buyers who agree to strict conservation easements. This keeps land on local property tax rolls and supports local government. Land trusts can also sell property to preservation organizations at less than the market price. The amount of value between the market price and the actual sale price is considered a donation to the organization for tax purposes. The Land Trust Alliance, founded in 1982, provides technical support to the growing panoply of land trusts in the U.S. They also take a National Land Trust Census that lists lands protected by state, local, and national land trusts. The last census in 2010 reported that land trusts protect 47 million acres of land in the U.S., double that recorded in the 2000 census. Land trusts were critical in doubling the size of the Hawaii Volcanoes National Park in 2003 and in the creation of the Great Sand Dunes National Park in Colorado in 2004. The Peninsula Open Space Trust (POST) in San Mateo County, south of San Francisco, is effectively expanding the Golden Gate National Recreation Area and San Mateo County Park network without government appropriations by buying key parcels and accepting easements on coastal farmland threatened by development.

Innovations in Park Management: The Presidio Trust

There have been many individual responses to the broad budgetary challenges facing parks in the United States. One of the most unique and successful innovations is underway within the GGNRA at the Presidio. Although the Presidio was included within the legislative boundary of the park in 1972, it was not transferred to the park until 1994, during a period of growing fiscal austerity in the United States. The 1,500-acre Presidio, designated a National Historic Landmark District in 1962, presented a special park stewardship challenge. The former army base shares the same peninsula as the bustling city of San Francisco, yet shelters 16 rare and endangered plant species within a complex landscape dotted with 800 buildings, more than 400 of which are historic, as well as the infrastructure of a small city. The post had suffered from decades of deferred maintenance. Revitalizing this national landmark would become the largest historic preservation project underway in the United States. The significant amount of capital needed to revitalize and operate the Presidio as a national park site precipitated a controversy in the United States Congress that nearly led to its sale in 1994.

A strategy for preserving the Presidio as a national park site without depending on federal appropriations was born out of this controversy when, in 1996, Congress created the Presidio Trust to preserve and enhance the Presidio working in partnership with the National Park Service. The Presidio Trust is a federal corporation guided by a presidentially appointed, seven-member board of directors, who set the direction and policies for transforming the Presidio into a vital place with historic, environmental, social, and academic significance. Public/private partnerships fund the rehabilitation of individual buildings and revitalize the Presidio. Each federal dollar invested in the Presidio was matched with four dollars from private or philanthropic sources, resulting in a combined $1.6 billion investment over 15 years. About 2,700 people now live

Previous pages: **The 1,491-acre Presidio of San Francisco**, a former military post now within the Golden Gate National Recreation Area, has an innovative management and funding model unique among national parks.
Robert Campbell, 2002, www. chamoismoon.com

44

in some 1,100 units of former military housing. Approximately 4,000 people work for a mix of some 200 for-profit and nonprofit organizations in rehabilitated Army buildings. After a 15-year transition period of decreasing congressional appropriations, the Presidio became financially self-sustaining in 2013. Had the Presidio not become a self-sustaining success by 2013, the land would have been sold off in pieces and developed, as described in the same legislation that established the Presidio Trust.

The creation of the Presidio Trust was the leading edge of a period of experimentation in new models for funding and governance of public sites with a similar mosaic of buildings and landscape. Similar experiments are now underway at Governor's Island in New York, Fort Monroe in Virginia, Sydney Harbour Trust in Australia, and a number of other sites across the United States and around the world.

National Park Challenges Today: External Threats and Baseline Inventories

The historic problem of arbitrary park boundaries within their larger ecosystems continues and is now intensified by the thickening of "exurban" development around many national parks. External threats to parks include air pollution (Grand Canyon and Great Smoky Mountains, among many others), water scarcity and pollution (Everglades), invasive species (many parks), and habitat fragmentation. Rising sea levels threaten sea-level shore parks. In many parks and monuments, there is insufficient knowledge of the condition of natural and cultural resources and inadequate inventories and baselines from which to

monitor change. Most archeological sites in the national park system, for example, have never been properly surveyed. In many places we do not even know what we are losing.

Forest Fires, Controlled Burns, and Exurban Development

For years, forest fires were suppressed in national parks despite the fact that thwarting the natural cycle of wildfires only builds up fuel for more destructive conflagrations later on. At Sequoia National Park, fire suppression halted the reproduction of the giant trees, which need fire to germinate their seeds. The Leopold Report of 1963 identified the role of fire in ecosystems and the damage that suppressing fire has created. In 1964, controlled burns were tried at Everglades and were successful. Forest management policy shifted in 1968 to continue controlled burns. Still, controlled burns can be controversial and occasionally get out of control. As exurban development spreads further and further away from cities and suburbs towards the borders of once-remote forests, there is countervailing pressure to suppress wildfires to protect real estate, in many cases expensive second homes.

Motorized Recreation

Changes in contemporary vehicle design and recreation also challenge parks. Off-road trucks and motorcycles can damage parks and are hard to police. "Empty" deserts are especially vulnerable to damage by mechanized vehicles. There is continual pressure from the manufacturers of motorized recreation, such as dirt bikes, all-terrain vehicles (ATVs), snowmobiles, and jet skies, to "open up" the parks to noisy machines that damage the ground, disturb wildlife habitats, and destroy the peace and quiet visitors seek in parks. Yellowstone is among the parks threatened by more snowmobiles. Cheaper ATVs are booming in popularity in rural areas. Some ATV enthusiasts like to ride in packs that scour the ground, trample vegetation, and kill wildlife. Some states, such as California, have created off-road vehicle parks to take the pressure off traditional parks.

Extreme Sports and Parks

The term "extreme sports" surfaced in the late 1980s and was first used for strenuous adult sports such as surfing, skydiving, rock climbing, skiing, snowboarding, mountain biking, hang gliding, white water kayaking, and bungee jumping, among others. With increased media exposure, extreme sports shifted to a younger generation, and now include skateboarding, aggressive inline skating, BMX (bicycle motocross), BASE jumping (jumping from a fixed object such as a cliff and using a parachute), downhill mountain biking, kite surfing, paragliding, parkour (free running), rock climbing, ice climbing, and downhill street luge (riding supine on a brakeless board down a public road). They appeal to counterculture youth, predominantly males. Extreme sports often involve speed, height, great physical exertion, or spectacular stunts. Stop-action photography and jump-cut video have popularized maneuvers that once were the preserve of professional Hollywood stuntmen. ESPN promoted the first Extreme Games in 1995, made-for-television events that advertisers relish in order to reach young consumers. Extreme sports tend to be solitary yet competitive activities. Imbued with an anarchic spirit, it is almost impossible by definition for parks to accommodate activities that aim to break all bounds. Parks and playing fields are not "extreme" spaces; in fact they are both precisely the opposite: *Rules* make

sports. Another defining characteristic of extreme sports is their high level of inherent danger. Participants often pit themselves against uncontrollable natural phenomena, including rough terrain, wind, snow, big waves, or high mountains. An accident or mistake can cause not just injury but death.

Extreme sports have obvious impacts on urban and national parks. Aggressive, downhill mountain bike racers are a hazard to hikers and destroy the tranquility of parks. Even hiking can be turned into an extreme activity. Today there are "extreme hikers" who rush over remote trails seeing how fast they can complete the hike while ignoring the natural world they are traversing and avoiding interaction with other hikers. In spectacular Yosemite Valley, as many as 60 rock climbers tackle El Capitan's 2,916 vertical feet of granite on a peak-season day. The new trend is speed: how *fast* can a climber scale the rock? Rock climbers wear out narrow footholds, and their steel pins in the rocks are permanent. Some climbers now BASE jump from the summit and parachute back down into the valley, even though this is illegal. At least 23 climbers have died in the attempt. Nationally, search and rescue operations cost the National Park Service about $5 million a year.

Guns in National Parks

Traditionally, firearms were not permitted in national parks. Ronald Reagan signed a law that allowed licensed gun owners to carry unloaded, disassembled firearms in the trunks of their cars in national parks. George W. Bush went further and allowed assembled, loaded guns in most national parks, but a federal judge put the new measure on hold. President Barack Obama signed a rider to a credit card bill

A **National Park Service guided hike** at the Fiery Furnace, Arches National Park, Utah.

NPS photo by Andrew Kuhn

in 2010 allowing licensed gun owners to bring firearms, including semiautomatic weapons, into national parks and wildlife refuges if weapons are allowed by the park's home state. In some cases, gun owners may bring concealed and loaded firearms into parks. However, it remains illegal to fire a weapon or kill an animal in national parks. In 2012, the House of Representatives passed the so-called Sportsmen's Heritage Act that would open much of the National Park System to hunting and recreational shooting. This proposal threatens the long heritage of national parks as sanctuaries for wildlife. Most national park rangers patrol unarmed. For seven consecutive years, park rangers have been the most assaulted federal law enforcement officers with the highest number of deaths. Allowing guns in parks makes all visitors more wary. It also undermines the sense of peace and security that park visitors seek.

Increasing Diversity in American Society and New Park Users

Some segments of U.S. society, such as African Americans, did not traditionally grow up with the idea that the national parks are for them or that the outdoors can be inspirational. People of color continue to be underrepresented among park visitors. Post-1965 changes in immigration law have resulted in increased ethnic diversity in the U.S. and this requires that national parks and monuments change their programming to better serve changing audiences. Making *all* Americans feel welcome in their parks can be fostered by outreach aimed at non-traditional audiences. Looking outward toward the larger, changing society requires a change in the deep-seated culture of the National Park Service. The National Park Service is diversifying its ranger force to better reflect the nation's racial, ethnic, gender, and sexual orientation diversity.

The "Wired" Generation, Virtual Reality, and Nature

National park visitation, measured as a per capita function of the national population, has been shrinking for nearly 30 years. The political base for parks needs to be expanded and deepened through the promotion of parks, something included in the Organic Act of 1916 that created the National Park Service but that the Park Service long thought was unnecessary. While ecology and environmentalism are now taught widely in schools, recent surveys indicate that youth today play outside less than previous generations did. Physical activity among many youths also seems to be declining, and obesity among the young and the general population is increasing alarmingly. Some observers such as William C. Tweed, the former chief naturalist at Sequoia and Kings Canyon National Parks, propose that the natural world means less to each succeeding generation. Some "wired" youngsters now prefer "virtual reality" to experiencing nature directly in parks. If true, this is an ominous development for both people and parks.

Climate Change and Other Global Threats

The consensus among scientists is that the earth and its atmosphere are getting warmer. From the long view of geologic time, this is not the first time this has happened. What is new is that global warming is happening within decades, not eons. Global warming is changing how some managers are thinking about the future of parks. Among the possible consequences of warming are extreme heat waves, increased wildland fires, more powerful hurricanes, coastal flooding, habitat destruction, and the extinction of flora and fauna. Some national parks are already experiencing the impact of global warming: Glaciers are melting, alpine habitats are becoming warmer climate zones, wildfires are larger and more frequent, and floods are increasing. Proposals to counter global warming by curtailing of CO_2 emissions through carbon taxes, cap-and-trade markets, or stiffer regulation spur opposition from vested economic interests, such as coal-dependant energy companies and coal mining regions. They and other anti-tax and "small government" groups deny the validity of the scientific consensus on global warming. In the 2012 presidential campaign, sensing the electorate's short-term priorities, neither candidate mentioned global warming and instead stressed increased production of traditional fossil fuels. Denial may work as an election strategy, but it ill prepares the nation for the fundamental economic and lifestyle changes that responding to global warming may entail.

Parks, Education, and Critical Connections

In 2001, the National Park System Advisory Board called upon the NPS to emphasize its mission as an *educator* by providing formal and informal programs for students and learners of all ages, both inside and outside park boundaries. On the historical side, the interpreters of national historical monuments are faced with growing historical illiteracy. Today Americans leave high school with little understanding of history or civics. Most U.S. colleges today do not require any history courses in their undergraduate programs. Mount Vernon conducted surveys and found that many young people did not know who George Washington was. A new visitor center was built to introduce the "Father of his Country" to the current generation. Historian David McCullough notes, "We are raising a generation of young Americans who are historically illiterate." This trend has obvious impacts on historical sites: Families stop coming. The feel-good, make-believe "history" of commercial theme parks threatens to displace real history, authentic sites, and the truth of human struggle.

Last but certainly not least, the all-important *relationship between human activity and environmental change* is rarely presented clearly in parks. Explaining the links between over-population, over-consumption, rampant pollution, habitat fragmentation, and the need for parks to preserve biodiversity is key. The U.S. National Park Service is now including information on climate change in its programs and publications. Parks and protected areas are now important not just for what they are, but also as classrooms for the planet.

Notes

1. *Preservation Magazine*, July–August, 2010, p. 29.

2. John Ise. *Our National Parks Policy: A Critical History.* Baltimore: Johns Hopkins Press, 1961, p. 17.

3. Ibid., pp. xii, 22.

4. Ibid., p. 48.

Chang Tang Nature Reserve

Nature Reserves, Wildlife, and Pastoralists in Tibet

George B. Schaller, Ph.D.
Wildlife Conservation Society, New York

This center of heaven,

This core of the earth,

This heart of the world,

Fenced round with snow,

The headland of all rivers,

Where the mountains are high and

The land is pure.

Tibetan poem, 8th–9th century

With its ecological wholeness, stark beauty, and sense of unfettered freedom, the Chang Tang is a place where mind and body can travel, where one's soul can dance.

The World's Second Largest Protected Reserve

A harsh, windswept landscape, remote and desolate, stretches across the northern part of the Tibetan Plateau in China. It is called the Chang Tang, the "northern plain," in Tibetan. It is 600 miles at its longest and 300 miles at its widest. It is the second largest protected reserve in the world, exceeded only by Greenland National Park. Much of this gaunt terrain lies 14,000 to 15,000 feet above sea level,

and its northern part is 16,000 to 17,000 feet high. Though austere, the Chang Tang has a tranquil beauty, its wild emptiness alluring with a sense of the unknown. The plains roll silently on, horizon giving way to horizon, broken by turquoise lakes and ice ranges with some peaks over 20,000 feet high. At this elevation, the vegetation is scant, grasses, forbs (herbaceous plants), and shrubs no more than a foot high. The climate is severe, to -40 degrees Fahrenheit (-40 Celsius) in winter. Snow falls even at the height of summer.

An alpine steppe covers the southern part of the Chang Tang, and with more precipitation here, alpine meadow extends over the eastern part. Here Tibetan

Left: **A lone wild yak bull**, weighing perhaps 1,500 pounds and with a mantle of hair hanging to his knees, overlooks his vast domain. (All photos this chapter are by the author.)

nomads live with their yaks, sheep, goats, and horses. The high northern area is desert steppe with the ground mostly bare, the scattered grass tufts too few to support livestock. In November and December 2006, a team of Tibetans, Han Chinese, and I drove cross-country west to east for 1,000 miles, a distance equivalent to that from New York to Chicago, and we did not see a single person. Yet there was a fair amount of wildlife, including Tibetan antelope or chiru, and wild yak. What a glorious experience! Where else in the world can one find its equal? The spirit exults that a wild place like this still exists.

With great foresight, the government of the People's Republic of China established the Chang Tang Nature Reserve in the Tibet Autonomous Region in 1993. At 115,000 square miles, it is the size of New Mexico or Italy. Other reserves border it in neighboring Xinjiang and Qinghai provinces, and together these offer a measure of protection to a Chang Tang area larger than California. Adjoining it to the east and extending beyond the Chang Tang is the 58,000-square-mile Sanjiangyuan Reserve created to protect the headwaters of China's great rivers— the Yellow, Yangtze, and Mekong—upon which the lives of millions of people in the lowlands depend. This vast protected region, still little known, represents one of the great natural treasures of China and the world. People live within the reserves in Tibet and Qinghai. The challenge is to manage the reserves in such a way that

Previous pages: **Chiru in search of forage** after an October blizzard that resulted in death by starvation of much wildlife and livestock.

Above: **Chiru males, singly and in small herds**, live largely segregated from females except during the mating season.

Following pages: **In June, most chiru females migrate north** in large herds for 100 to 200 miles to remote calving grounds, then return south to better grazing grounds. The Aru Range in the western Chang Tang, with peaks to 20,000 feet, looms beyond turquoise lakes.

the wildlife, rangelands, and communities all flourish. The conflicting demands of conservation, economic development, and the welfare of an indigenous culture need equal attention.

The Riches of the Chang Tang

At first glance the Chang Tang may seem barren, but it has a rich flora and fauna that have evolved in these harsh conditions. Over 300 species of flowering plants grow here, grasses and legumes and composites, as well as gentians, potentillas, asters, and many others. A bird list may reach 100 species, from black-necked cranes and bar-headed geese to sacker falcons, ravens, snow finches, and horned larks. The mammals comprise a unique

assemblage, one that first brought me to the Chang Tang. There is the chiru, the Tibetan antelope, whose migrations define the ecosystem. The wild yak, the rare and huge ancestor of the domestic yak, is to me the symbol of these remote uplands. The russet-colored Tibetan wild ass or kiang is widespread on good pastures; it is a curious creature that at times gallops parallel to passing vehicles. Others include the blue sheep—actually related to the goat—in rugged terrain, the graceful Tibetan gazelle, the Tibetan argali sheep with its massive curled horns, and, in the east, scattered herds of white-lipped deer. Preying on these ungulates are the wolf, snow leopard, and lynx. Newborns fall prey at times to red fox, Tibetan sand fox, and

Tibetan brown bear. All these predators also hunt the small plateau pika, which is locally abundant and remains active around its burrows all year.

To study this diverse mammal community and to promote its protection has drawn me back to the Chang Tang every year for over a quarter century. Even to locate the mysterious calving grounds to which chiru females migrate as far as 200 miles in the most desolate and uninhabited terrain requires a major expedition. No wildlife population remains static. A

heavy snowstorm may starve thousands of animals, domestic as well as wild, as I witnessed in October 1985. Commercial hunting greatly reduced wild populations in the 1990s, but with better protection, numbers in some areas are again increasing. But greater numbers of some species such as kiang and bear create human-wildlife conflict. And as the nomad culture changes with improvements in economic conditions, attitudes toward and tolerance of wildlife change, too. Conservation is not a goal measured in a limited project but is a never-ending

Villagers in the western Chang Tang circle a chorten or stupa—a receptacle for offerings in Buddhism—in a clockwise direction, a daily ritual for many.

Above right: **Tibetan nomads** have traditionally killed wildlife for subsistence. This mother has her swaddled infant in a cradle made of kiang hide.

Below right: **A high-ranking lama**, the head of a monastery, blesses Tibetan villagers at a festival. Most communities have an annual summer festival, but this one was also devoted to conservation, to living in harmony with the land according to Buddhist principles.

process to which my Chinese co-workers and I have dedicated ourselves and to which we have to adapt continually.

The Chang Tang Reserve is contiguous with the West Kunlun, Mid-Kunlun, and Arjin Shan reserves in Xinjiang, and with the Kekexili Reserve in Qinghai. The Chang Tang Reserve is thus not just a limited protected area or national park, but together with the other reserves represents a whole landscape, an ecosystem in which all species of plants and animals can continue to seek their

destiny. Climate change will affect or is already affecting all protected areas. As habitats shift or are modified, species can adapt, move, or die. The Chang Tang ecosystem is large and varied enough that species can accommodate themselves to changes, if properly managed. Smaller reserves, by contrast, will be able to survive only by establishing one or more strictly protected core areas, such as national parks, surrounded by a landscape managed to assure the livelihood of people as well as all other species, and with core areas connected by corridors of

habitat through which species can move from one area to another.

We know that the Chang Tang's riches are not measured in oil and gold—though both occur there—but in its spacious vistas, cushions of flowers, vibrant chiru herds, and distinctive pastoral culture. All these must remain a gift to the future.

Do if you like that which may seem sinful
But help living beings,
Because that is truly pious work.
—*The last words of Tibetan hermit saint Milarepa (1052–1135)*

The Pastoralists Past and Present
Tibetan nomads, best referred to as pastoralists, evoke the romantic illusion that they have always been free to roam with their livestock in search of their destiny. Not so. For centuries pastoralists were bound by heredity to an area controlled by a monastery or an aristocratic family to whom they paid annual taxes in butter, wool, and meat. Tibet's old society came to an end in 1959, and a decade later, with the onset of China's Cultural Revolution, private property was abolished and cooperatives were established. These were disbanded in 1981 after causing extreme hardship. Property including livestock was then redistributed equally to families, and areas were divided into administrative units or *xiang* within which households had grazing rights.

Historically, pastures were reallocated every three years. Their size depended on the number of livestock. This important practice was discontinued in 1959 with the result that many pastures were seriously overgrazed, especially since the government promoted livestock expansion. Then, in the 1990s, the government again changed grazing policy. Each family was given a parcel of land with a lease of 30 to 70 years, depending on the area, to which the family was confined. Because the human population has increased greatly in recent decades, there was not enough land to give a sizable plot to everyone, and some families received too little to support themselves. Nomads had now become small-time ranchers. During a drought or heavy snow the livestock could not usually be moved elsewhere to better grazing. As a result, pastures became ever more degraded, a trend accelerated by climate change, which has brought more frequent and more violent sandstorms and changes in precipitation.

Since the pastoralists now "owned" land, they wanted to fence it, just as settlers did in North America and Australia. Fences, subsidized by the government, keep stray livestock out—and wildlife, too—and the owner's livestock confined without the need to herd it. And this places ever greater stress on the fragile pastures. As

Above left: **In spite of a severe climate**, summer in the Chang Tang offers a palate of bright flowers, such as these asters, yellow-flowered cinquefoil (*Potentilla*), and white-flowered cushion plants (*Androsace*).

Above right: **All vegetation in the windy, arid Chang Tang** hugs the ground, such as this red-berried *Ephedra* and white-leafed *Leontopodium*.

A legume of the genus *Oxytropis* after a hailstorm.

Right: **A plateau pika sits at its burrow entrance.** Extremely abundant in places, the diminutive pika is a "keystone" species in the Chang Tang, a key to soil fertility and plant diversity by its digging, and a source of food for all avian and mammalian predators. Pastoralists and government departments wrongly claim that pikas compete too much for forage with livestock, and consequently they have been poisoned over a huge area of the eastern Chang Tang.

Below right: **A pair of Tibetan snowcock,** a six-pound gallinaceous bird unique to the Tibetan Plateau, with newborn chicks.

Sangjie, a nomad, told me, "The largest problem we face is changes in ourselves."

The pastoralists began to settle down in the late 1980s. The traditional yak-hair tents have mostly now given way to mud-brick houses. As economic conditions improved, families bought motorcycles to replace horses. Today houses, and even tents, may have solar panels and satellite dishes to run television sets and electric blenders to mix the traditional butter tea. New roads permit trucks to deliver grain and other necessities to remote households and to buy wool, butter, and hides. This has eliminated the ancient trading caravans.

I have witnessed these rapid changes. Tibetan pastoralists adapted to live in one of the world's harshest environments, and they remain resilient even in the face of recent political changes. They are hospitable and generous and concerned about the land and their future. I admire them greatly.

The Endangered Chiru

We walked for a week in 1997 across the steppe in western Qinghai province. The rangeland was in good condition and people were few, but we looked for wildlife in vain. The chiru, yak, kiang, and others had been slaughtered by local people and outsiders to "become rich," as one Tibetan explained. As we studied wildlife in the Chang Tang during the 1990s, we observed the past die as the wild herds were butchered to feed laborers in town and to make a quick profit. The chiru suffered the most. Trapped by pastoralists and gunned down by motorized teams from the towns, tens of thousands were slaughtered for their wool, the finest of any species. Smuggled to Kashmir in India, the wool was there woven into soft, luxurious shahtoosh, a product that is much in demand as a fashion statement by the world's wealthy. A beautifully embroidered shawl may sell for $15,000. The horns of the chiru are widely used in traditional medicine and find a ready market in Lhasa and Beijing. Although

The wolf is the top predator in the Chang Tang, where it hunts alone or in small packs. It is hated by pastoralists because of its predation on livestock, but here it is dining on a female chiru.

Right: **The snow leopard, distributed sparsely** but widely in rugged terrain, is to me the icon of these mountains but disliked by pastoralists because it preys at times on livestock. Its ultimate survival would reveal our tolerance, respect, and compassion for all species, as well as our concern for a healthy and harmonious mountain environment.

the trade is wholly illegal, I estimate that as many as 250,000 to 300,000 chiru were killed during the 1990s. Better protection in China and enforcement of wildlife trade laws in other countries have greatly reduced the carnage. Indeed, our surveys show that some chiru populations are increasing in number, protected by local officials and communities. Perhaps someday the chiru can be harvested in a sustainable manner for their meat and wool to benefit Tibetan communities. Good science and good laws are essential for conservation—but are not enough. To achieve success, local communities must be involved. They must be partners in any endeavor, contributing their knowledge, insights, and skills, as well as their moral values.

The Challenges of the Chang Tang

About a decade ago, the government confiscated guns from the local population, something that greatly benefited wildlife. However, protection may create new problems, as two

examples illustrate. Kiang have become so abundant in some places that pastoralists complain about competition with their livestock for grass. Brown bears used to be shot when they killed livestock or entered an isolated tent. In the past few years they have learned that houses are safe and offer free meals of butter, flour, and meat. When no one is home, a bear smashes windows, doors, or even the wall to ransack the rooms. In some areas bears are raising such havoc that people are losing patience. We have to work with communities and government to help resolve such problems through research, education, imaginative joint solutions, and better wildlife and livestock management policies.

Then there is the problem of the pikas, an essential link in the food chain of the Chang Tang. Weighing only 4 to 6 ounces, these tiny relatives of rabbits can become extremely abundant. Pastoralists and officials despise pikas because the perception is that they compete heavily

The Tibetan brown bear is a unique subspecies confined to the Tibetan Plateau. After the government confiscated most guns, the bears began to break into unoccupied houses of pastoralists in search of food such as butter, flour, and meat.

A poacher stands with his rifle by a pile of frozen chiru carcasses and severed chiru heads. The horns are sold for decorations in homes or ground into traditional Chinese medicines; the wool from the hides, the finest in the world, is illegally exported to India to be woven into expensive shahtoosh shawls for the international fashion market.

with livestock for forage and destroy pastures. As a result, they have been mass-poisoned in an eradication program covering over 80,000 square miles. But do they really damage rangelands? Research shows that pikas become most abundant on degraded pastures, just as prairie dogs do in North America. Their digging brings minerals to the surface, making plants more nutritious and diverse around burrows. Soil loosened by pikas holds water better and promotes plant growth, again a benefit to livestock. Pikas eat some poisonous plants that can kill sheep or goats. Snow finches nest inside old burrows, and the whole predator guild from weasel to bear to golden eagle preys on pikas. These and other benefits are of immense value to the whole ecological community of the Chang Tang. Animals are a tangle of fact, cultural ideas, and illusions. We are trying to change perceptions through community meetings and with a booklet on the importance of pikas, written in Tibetan for adults and schoolchildren alike.

Three points have to be considered. One is that problems are local and must be solved locally. A second point is that no single approach may offer universal solutions. And a third point is that all such problems are biologically and culturally so complex that they require a long-term integrated approach. There is as yet no wildlife management on the Tibetan Plateau, not even in the reserves. Animals are either fully protected or completely unprotected. There is no policy to resolve human-wildlife conflict, nor one to manage species in a rational and sustainable manner.

Presently, we address problems on a case-by-case basis. Pastoralists are fencing the critical winter pastures to save the grass for their livestock. Fences hinder movement of wildlife, and kiang, chiru, and gazelle sometimes die when they become entangled in the wire. We are working with communities to design fences that cause the least amount of hindrance, and we are trying various methods of bear-proofing homes.

Spiritual Values and the Future of the Chang Tang

There is now, in general, a much greater awareness of the value of wildlife and a healthy habitat on the Tibetan Plateau than there was even two decades ago. Among the governmental organizations involved in studying and protecting the Chang Tang and other reserves are the State Forestry Administration, the State Environmental Protection Agency, the forestry departments of Tibet, Qinghai, and Xinjiang, the Institute of Zoology of the Chinese Academy of Sciences, the Northwest Plateau Institute of Biology, the Tibet Academy of Agricultural and Animal Sciences, and the Tibet Plateau Institute of Biology. Non-governmental conservation organizations are also making valuable contributions, including the Snowland Great Rivers Environmental Protection Association, Green River, Shan Shui Conservation Center, World Wildlife Fund, and Wildlife Conservation Society. Some Tibetan communities themselves are beginning to maintain the ecological integrity of their land. To give one example, the community of Cuochi in Qinghai banned hunting because of the belief that the deities of the nearby holy mountain Morvudan Zha will punish the people if they kill wildlife. The community now prohibits livestock grazing on one small mountain range to protect wild yak, provides rangeland where chiru can feed unmolested in winter, and monitors wildlife populations.

Preliminary management plans have been prepared for the Chang Tang and some other reserves. Both the national and local governments provide funds, though not enough, to maintain a guard force, conduct wildlife surveys, regulate livestock numbers, and develop other management initiatives. But since ultimately the local communities will determine the fate of wildlife and rangelands, conservation organizations have initiated education programs, organized village patrols to deter outsiders from poaching, and have encouraged an attitude of caring for the environment—and ultimately the region's own future.

Monasteries have sacred lands where hunting is forbidden. We have been working with monks to show them how to monitor and record wildlife, and also to encourage the communities near them to live by the basic Buddhist principles of respect, love, and compassion for all living beings. We hope that with ecological insight and religious conviction local communities will realize that their livelihood depends on treating their land with understanding and restraint. To that end, we also encourage festivals presided over by a revered lama (Tibetan Buddhist monk) who speaks about the importance of people, livestock, and wildlife living together in harmony. There is dancing and horse-racing, and then everyone ascends the lower slopes of the holy mountain (each community has one). There the lama blesses the land and all life as an eternal gift to the future.

Previous pages: **A daily task for a pastoral family,** no matter what the weather, is to herd and guard flocks of domestic sheep and goats, driving the animals to the best pastures and guarding them from wolves, snow leopards, and other predators.

Where to Learn More

BOOKS

Melvyn and Cynthia Beal Goldstein. *Nomads of Western Tibet: The Survival of a Way of Life*. Berkeley, Calif.: University of California Press, 1990.

Rick Ridgeway. *The Big Open*. Washington D.C.: National Geographic Society, 2004.

George Schaller. *Tibet's Hidden Wilderness*. New York: Harry N. Abrams, 1997.

George Schaller. *Wildlife of the Tibetan Steppe*. Chicago: University of Chicago Press, 1998.

VIDEOS

These are about the killing of chiru for their wool to make illegal shahtoosh shawls:
Deadly Fashion. National Geographic Television.

Eco-Heroes, Chang Tang Reserve. Disney.

Enforcers: Fish and Wildlife Service. History Channel.

FILM

Mountain Patrol—Kekexili. Filmed in the Chang Tang by a Hong Kong company and based on fact.

NONPROFIT ORGANIZATIONS

Wildlife Conservation Society. www.wcs. org/saving-wild-places/asia/chang-tang-china.aspx. 2300 Southern Blvd., Bronx, NY, 10460

Also, www.baohu.org/en/ (in English and Chinese). Beijing office: Institute of Zoology Chinese Academy of Sciences, Datunlu, Chaoyang District, Beijing 100101

Center for Nature and Society and Shan Shui Conservation Center, Peking University
www.shansui.org, www.wildpanda.org (in Chinese but soon also in English) Conservation Biology Building, College of Life Sciences, Peking University, Beijing 100871

Panthera, leaders in wildcat conservation. www.panthera.org
8 W. 40th St., New York, NY 10018

World Wildlife Fund. www.worldwildlife. org
1250 24th St., N.W., Washington, DC 20090

How to Get Involved

Know the issues and be alert.

Report illegal wildlife trade to the U.S. Fish and Wildlife Service.

Write to involved organizations so that they can forward correspondence to local officials or discuss matters with them directly. Donate funds to concerned nonprofit organizations.

If you visit the Tibetan Plateau, inquire about progress in conservation. This alerts officials that there is worldwide interest in the Chang Tang.

Serengeti National Park and Ngorongoro Conservation Area, Tanzania

Prospects, Problems, and Progress

John F. R. Bower, Ph.D.
University of California, Davis

Audax Z. Mabulla
University of Dar es Salaam, Tanzania

The Serengeti National Park, Tanzania, and the adjacent Ngorongoro Conservation Area were established mainly for the purpose of protecting one of the world's most extraordinary concentrations of migratory and resident wildlife. However, the Ngorongoro Conservation Area is also home to a substantial population of Maasai, a livestock-herding people who move throughout the Ngorongoro Area in search of pasture and water for their cattle and small stock. The combined Serengeti/Ngorongoro region is also a major tourist destination containing numerous lodges, tented campsites, and other facilities, as well as an extensive network of game-viewing tracks throughout the region.

Within the Serengeti/Ngorongoro area are many archeological sites that document parts of the entire span of human prehistory, from the earliest Stone Age to the Iron Age. These include not only important excavated sites, such as Olduvai Gorge investigated by the renowned Leakey family, but also dozens of sites known only from surface finds, and therefore requiring excavation to expose their record of human biological and cultural evolution. Unfortunately, the region's unexcavated archeological record, while showing great potential for deepening our understanding of the human career, is at present the "Achilles' heel" of regional archeology. What is involved is nothing less than destruction of archeological sites as a result of providing water for Maasai pastoralist's flocks in the Ngorongoro Conservation Area and construction activities within the combined parks, such as road building and repair.

While the need for these pursuits is beyond question, the archeological consequences can be devastating. This is clearly revealed by damage evident at the few known occurrences of site destruction. One of these is a site with excellent preservation and scientific potential that was quarried for road gravel, resulting in the removal of all but a trace of the archeological content as sad testimonial to the site's demise.

Equally deplorable is the destruction of a site in the Ngorongoro Conservation Area that contained 3.6 million-year-old footprints documenting the dawn of human upright posture and bipedal locomotion, as contrasted with the quadrupedal locomotion of our nearest living relatives, the ape, including such African species as chimpanzees and gorillas. Thus, the advent of bipedalism

Left: **Long-billed bee-eater.**
Photo by Susan Hoffman

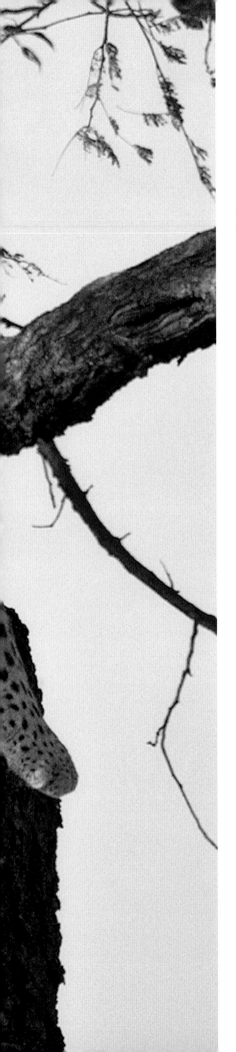

is believed to mark the separation of the human lineage from nonhuman relatives—a major inflection point in human evolution on which the now famous Laetoli footprints have the potential to shed great light.

The Serengeti Park and associated Ngorongoro Conservation Area are endowed with a vast wealth of natural and cultural resources, all of which call for careful management, including not only attention to the various interests of tourism, Maasai herders, and archeologists, but also to conflicting goals among them. Dealing with such conflicts will involve resolving a tangled web of encounters among herders, park staff, and archeologists.

Serengeti Wildlife

The combined Serengeti National Park/ Ngorongoro Conservation Area is one of the most popular tourist destinations in the world due to the extraordinary variety and number of animals that inhabit the area. These include not only predators such as cheetahs, but also a broad assortment of herbivores, such as the zebra, wildebeest, elephant, African Cape buffalo, giraffe, baboon, tortoise, and hippopotamus. Bird watchers are entertained by a wide variety of species, including mobs of flamingos and numerous highly colorful birds, such as the long-billed bee-eater.

Maasai Pastoralists

Cattle, valued mainly for their milk, are the nutritional mainstay of the Maasai people. But herding livestock can be challenging in the Ngorongoro Conservation Area, where large carnivores, such as lions, threaten the livestock, thereby necessitating protection by young men of warrior status. For herding cultures, access to abundant water is essential, sometimes requiring long, daily marches from base settlement to water source and back. Herders sometimes excavate for subsurface water. While this practice is generally harmless, in some cases it damages archeological remains of great importance.

Left: **Predators are a constant threat** to the livestock of the Maasai.
Photo by Robert W. Floerke

Previous pages: **Zebras, waterfowl, wildebeests and flamingos.**
Photo by Susan Hoffman

Above: **Elephants and tourist vehicles.**
Photo by Robert W. Floerke

Left: **Women with infant and dwelling.** In the arid conditions of the Ngorongoro region, family-sized dwellings with dry mud covering are sufficient for year-round habitation by small family units. The units are polygamous, and young children are attached to their mothers. Young adult males of warrior age lead an essentially bachelor existence until they become eligible for marriage.
Photo by Jan Bower

Above: **Herder and cattle.**

Right: **A Maasai warrior.**

Photo Jan Bower

Tourism and Its Impacts

No one can doubt the importance of tourism to Tanzania's economy. Nor is there any question about the need for water in the Maasai pastoral economy. Yet both tourism and Maasai pastoralism have inadvertently contributed to the endangerment, even destruction, of important archeological material. Unfortunately, the global fame of the Serengeti wildlife has jeopardized its less well-known archeological record. In most cases the damage is indirect, stemming in part from Maasai unfamiliarity with archeology and their inability to recognize archeological material. Until recently, the park staff was equally uninformed on archeology, and therefore unprepared to protect it. The construction of tourist lodges and roads to accommodate park visitors has often resulted in the destruction of archeological sites, a development that initially drew a shrug of the shoulders. However, recent park managers have shown a heightened concern for cultural heritage management in order to minimize archeological destruction.

Top right: The Serengeti Sopa Lodge.

Photo Jan Bower

Right: **Olduvai Gorge's "Zinjanthropus" find-site.** In addition to the park's virtually unlimited game-viewing possibilities, there are opportunities for visiting world famous archeological sites, such as the find-spot of one of the earliest bipedal human ancestors.

Photo by Jan Bower

Below right: **The massive flow of tourism in the park** sometimes overwhelms the park's facilities.

Photo by Robert W. Floerke

Left: **Archeologists examine a site** whose contents have been disturbed by the extraction of gravel for road building. An unknown number of sites have been destroyed as a result of quarrying for road metal in deposits that contain archeological sites. The threat of a road across the northern part of the park might have proven fatal to the renowned Serengeti migration. Fortunately, the north road project was abandoned because of increased internal pressure and lobbying by environmental activists. However, the possibility of road building across the migration route remains a potent threat.
Photo by Jan Bower

Where to Learn More

BOOKS

Kay Turner (wife of Myles Turner, a Serengeti park warden). *Serengeti Home.* New York: Dial Press, 1977.

Bernard and Michael Grzimek. *Serengeti Shall Not Die.* New York: Ballantine Books, 1973. A classic that is readily accessible to a general audience.

Mary Leakey. *Disclosing the Past, An Autobiography.* New York: McGraw Hill, 1986.

Craig Packer. *Into Africa.* Chicago: The University of Chicago Press, 1994. By a specialist on lions, which he has studied intensively in the Serengeti Park.

Richard Potts. *Early Hominid Activities at Olduvai.* Piscataway, N.J.: Transaction Publishers, 2010. A technical volume that contains impressive and abundant content accessible to anyone seriously interested in the lives of some of the earliest ancestors of existing human populations.

Donald Johanson and Blake Edgar. *From Lucy to Language.* New York: Simon & Schuster Editions, 1996. Written for the general reader and beautifully illustrated.

Tepilit Ole Saitoti. *The Worlds of a Maasai Warrior.* Berkeley, Calif.: University of California Press, 1988. An unusual outlook on wild animal preservation derived from the author's Maasai upbringing.

PERIODICAL LITERATURE

Audax Z. P. Mabulla and John R. F. Bower. "Cultural Heritage Management in Tanzania's Protected Areas: Challenges and Future Prospects" in *CRM: The Journal of Heritage Stewardship*, Vol. 7, Number 1, Winter 2010.

WEBSITES

African Wildlife Foundation: www.awf.org

Maasai People: www.maasai-association.org

Tanzania National Parks Official Site: www.tanzaniaparks.com

Serengeti Official Site: www.serengeti.org

Smithsonian Institution: www.humanorigins.si.edu

Above: **The Loiyangalani archeological team** in the Serengeti National Park.
Photo by Jan Bower

IF YOU VISIT

The annual, massive migration of wildlife in the Serengeti Park takes place during the long rainy season (March and April), but the park contains huge numbers of animals throughout the year.

Olduvai is a deep gorge measuring 30 miles long and 295 feet deep, whose exposed deposits contain fossil fauna, hominid remains, and artifacts, ranging from more than 2 million years ago to historic time. A small museum offers on-site lectures.

A Maasai village near the Ngorongoro Crater presents opportunities for photography, purchasing art and jewelry, and observing the traditional dress and lifeway of the Maasai people.

The Visitors Information Center inside the Serengeti Park gives excellent detail on both the wildlife and archeology of the park.

National Archeological Parks of Pompeii, Herculaneum, Stabiae, Boscoreale, and Oplontis, Italy

Mass Tourism, Pleasures, and Politics in the Shadow of Vesuvius

Judith Harris
Archeological Journalist, Rome

Left: **The Roman aesthetic placed a premium on literal depictions of nature**, and in light wells called viridaria at a luxurious seaside villa at Oplontis, near Pompeii, the walls were decorated with frescos of carefully detailed plants, fountains and birds, like the one in this birdbath. This villa, which had ample gardens and a huge swimming pool, may have belonged to the family of Nero's second wife, Poppaea Sabina.

The Archeological Riches of the Gulf of Naples

Ever since the Bronze Age some 4,000 years ago, diverse cultures have prospered in the fertile territory of the Gulf of Naples with its rich soil and mild climate. Early Pompeii, overlooking the mouth of the sole river emptying into the splendid bay, was visited by seafaring Greeks and Phoenicians. Around 800 B.C.E., inland Oscan tribesmen founded a farming village there. Later the town fell under the dominion of Etruscans and Greeks from Cumae up the coast. In the fifth century B.C.E., Oscan-speaking Samnites from the interior conquered Pompeii. The city was successfully besieged after 89 B.C.E. by the Roman general Sulla. He granted his veterans allotments inside the city walls. The town was enriched under the Romans by sales of the abundant regional wheat crop and local wine. It also shared in ship building and repairs for the Imperial Roman fleet. Ancient artifacts continue to be uncovered almost everywhere holes are dug in and around Naples. More riches lie underwater, including building ruins and shipwrecks.

Destruction and Discovery

High on a lava plateau, Pompeii began as a Bronze Age village, one of several destroyed by a devastating eruption of Vesuvius around 1800 B.C.E. For over 1,400 years the volcano lay dormant and the town was gradually reoccupied. A major earthquake in 62 C.E. damaged half of Roman Pompeii, and many citizens, particularly the wealthiest, moved away. Repairs and remodeling were still underway on August 24 of 79 C.E. when the eruption of Vesuvius buried the city and shoved the shoreline a quarter mile into the bay.

In 1709, Herculaneum became the first Vesuvian site to be excavated. Deep tunnels were cut into rock-hard layers of lava and tuff (solidified volcanic mud). Pompeii was discovered in 1744, and, because it was shallowly buried under a light blanket of pumice pebbles, excavation was easier and faster there. Excavations at Oplontis, on the seashore near Pompeii, began in the 18th century but were abandoned until restarted in earnest in 1964. Digs, both scientific and clandestine, continue in the region. Illegal excavations that fuel the black market

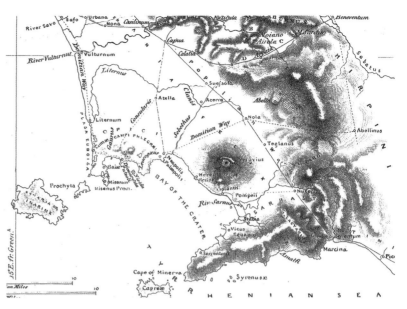

in antiquities are a severe problem in southern Italy and Sicily.

High and Low: A Complete Record of Roman Life

It was as if the clock stopped in August 79 C.E. The shroud of volcanic debris destroyed Pompeii, but also preserved the city that is today recognized as unique in offering a snapshot of daily life in antiquity. The 18th century inaugurated the first phase of archeological activity, treasure hunting for great works of art to embellish first personal and later the royal collection in Naples. At the outset many lesser frescos were accidentally and even deliberately destroyed. No records were kept of where things were found. Change came with the advent of scientific archeology, born at Pompeii in the late 18th century. From the mid-19th century onward, excavators have recorded and published their findings.

At present, further digging at Pompeii is not permitted. Archeologists there prefer to focus on the maintenance of what is visible today and to await further high-tech advances in non-invasive archeology. However, some sites, including inland ones, are being excavated today. At Pompeii teams of archeologists from many nations are reviewing and revising older research. Others are sinking narrow test pits that permit them to map the earliest streets under the Roman city. At Herculaneum there is some pressure to expand the excavations toward the still-buried Basilica.

Green Spaces Within the Ruins

Romans loved gardens, both real and in frescos.

The Greek-inspired rear garden in a fine villa was called a peristyle, a square or

Previous pages: **In this aerial view of Pompeii**, the Roman Forum is near the center of the walled city and Mount Vesuvius on the horizon. West of the ruins is the modern city of Pompei spread over five square miles, with 30,000 residents. *Public domain*

Top: **This remarkably accurate view of the Gulf of Naples**, with volcanic Mount Vesuvius in the center, was made by English architect William Gell and published in 1832 in London. The map shows the city situated between the mountainous Sorrentine Peninsula (bottom) and the volcano. William Gell and John P. Gandy, *Pompeiana: The Topography, Edifices and Ornaments of Pompeii, The Results of Excavations since 1819* (London: 1832) / Judith Harris

Above: **Joseph Wright of Derby, *Vesuvius from Portici*** (c. 1775). Oil on canvas. Although British

painter Wright never saw Mount Vesuvius erupt, he heard descriptions of the particularly violent explosion that had taken place three years before he visited Naples in 1773. Wright was an early student of the scientific effects of light and made some 30 paintings of the volcano erupting, seen solely in his imagination.
Huntington Library, Pasadena, California

Above: **In 1998, British architect Nicholas Wood painted this reconstruction** of the small peristyle decorated with fresco paintings and sculptures in the House of the Tragic Poet, discovered at Pompeii in 1824. Pompeiian townhouses such as this combined the traditional Italic house with the Greek or Hellenistic architectural tradition. Exterior walls had few or no windows, so inner courtyards provided light and air. The Roman entry was an atrium whose square roof hole (compluvium) stood atop a square rainwater basin (impluvium). From the Greek architectural tradition came the separate rear garden, or peristyle, often surrounded by a colonnaded walkway. Edward Bulwer Lytton used this house as a setting for his 1834 novel, *The Last Days of Pompeii*.
Courtesy Nicholas Wood, architect

rectangular space bordered by a covered walkway or portico. In the Pompeiian town house—a scaled-down version of a villa—the peristyle often had a decorative wall fountain or pool and scattered statuary. Flowering oleanders, grape arbors, and fig, apple, lemon, and cypress trees offered shade. Borders bloomed with bay bushes, acanthus, box hedges, roses, ivy, medicinal herbs, and flowers for perfumes. Charred stumps and pollen traces tell archeobotanists about these gardens, further described in fresco paintings. Fashionable because houses had few windows and hence dark rooms, these delightful frescos show such details as birds, marble fountains, painted stone fence posts, and the latticed wooden fencing that lined garden paths.

Today, maintenance of the archeological park's green spaces requires extensive and cautious hand work, including pruning and removal of the weeds that sprout from the walls of the ruins. Winter freezes expand their roots, weakening masonry. Chemical weed killers are a problem, however, because they contain ingredients that could damage painted walls still buried underground.

250 Years of Exposure

Within the ring of city walls, themselves requiring maintenance to prevent collapse, are thousands of ruined buildings—private houses, temples, baths, shops, apartment buildings—with tens of thousands of roofless rooms and hundreds of thousands of fragile wall and floor surfaces. Lacking roofs, their stone- and stucco-covered brick walls were never meant to be exposed to the elements. Some buildings have been exposed to the weather—which now includes acid rain and chemical pollution—for well over two centuries. Sunlight and rain fade frescos, which are also a target of tourist graffiti. Winter freezes, vandalism, and the pounding of millions of footsteps disintegrate exposed mosaic floors. A lake of lava underlies the whole area, and Pompeii is subject to constant tremors that further stress walls and buildings. An earthquake in 1980 weakened many ruins.

Many Pompeiian houses have been restored several times in less than a century on the basis of changing criteria. The first restoration of the now-collapsed House of the Gladiators was necessary after mistaken Allied bombing during World War II. In the 1950s, a cement roof was added to that house but proved too heavy for the ancient walls. When the winter of 2010–2011 brought the greatest amount of rain in 280 years, the embankments against which many ancient buildings lean was weakened. That rainfall contributed to the collapse of the House of the Gladiators, as well as to a mudslide that damaged the House of the Chaste Lovers.

Opposite, top: **These body casts in the garden of the House of the Cryptoporticus** date from the 1890s. Archeologists have found evidence of 1,047 victims inside the city out of a population of as many as 20,000, including an estimated 2,000 slaves. Many who fled the first, lighter surge of volcanic dust died outside the city from later blasts of 932° F (500° C) heat. The bodies of humans and animals encased in pyroclastic material eventually disintegrated, leaving hollows in the hardened volcanic debris. The mid-19th century park superintendent, archeologist Giuseppe Fiorelli, had plaster of Paris poured into the hollows, in which casts were made. Today, plastic resin is used.

Soprintendenza Archeologica di Pompei

Opposite, middle: **Initially few skeletal remains had been found** at Herculaneum, leading archeologists to assume that most inhabitants of that resort town had escaped. But after 1980, when the original waterfront was discovered, some 300 skeletons of individuals of all ages were found. Because cremation was the practice in ancient Rome, the discoveries allowed paleopathologists to advance knowledge of everything from fluoride in teeth to illnesses suffered by the families of Herculaneum.

Photo by David Willey

Opposite, bottom: **The long Via dell'Abbondanza**, shown here in a photograph from the 1870s, was Pompeii's main street. Many of Pompeii's 100 townhouses had doorways opening onto it, but it also had countless shops and a few workplaces, as well as fast-food stalls of every level, from those decorated with costly marble facing to simple stands.

Giacomo Brogi, Edizioni Brogi, Florence / Randolph Delehanty

Above: **Within the walls of ancient Pompeii.** At the top right, with the white entrance, is a newly restored building slated to become a museum. Visible to the left is a metal roof typical of the protective covering needed at especially fragile sites such as this one.

Photo by David Willey

Parks at Risk

A 1997 law granted Pompeii fiscal independence, and the site generates about 20 million euros ($25 million) a year from tickets and concessions. Nevertheless problems remain unresolved, and provisions for both ordinary maintenance and programmed conservation are woefully inadequate. Although in the past few years over $160 million was spent on restorations, under $3 million of this was budgeted for maintenance, and the last trained archeologist was hired 11 years ago. To provide better visitor amenities like restrooms is difficult, yet an expensive new visitors' facility has never opened, reportedly due to lack of connection with the electrical grid. Sponsored by the World Monument Fund, *Un Piano per Pompei* and a geo-referenced database mapped the building types and conditions in the park between 1997 and 2002. But the master plan ended abruptly in 2006 when that funding was not renewed.

Declaring the park in an official "state of emergency," in February 2009 the government of Silvio Berlusconi shifted Pompeii's management from the Cultural Heritage Ministry's control to a special commissioner of the national Civil Protection Agency responsible solely to Berlusconi. This emergency status declaration allowed the bypassing of normal bidding procedures.

As in many another country, the new commissioner's public relations team went fishing for a promotional slogan and came up with POMPEIVIVA (Pompeii lives). Needlessly costly gates installed throughout the ruins repeat this marketing slogan. They replaced inexpensive simple wooden barriers. Other senseless projects ensued, including multimedia programs at the Domus dei Casti Amanti and Domus

di Iulius Polibius. What some critics call dumb and wasteful were part of the so-called emergency "entertainment archeology" campaign. Another element was "Adopt a Dog," an expensively launched effort to rid the site of the dogs traditionally cared for by guards. The campaign boomeranged when unwanted dogs were dumped in the park.

Clustered outside the entrance to the park are stalls selling fresh orange juice, snacks, and souvenirs, many operated by the same families for generations. They came under attack but fortunately have survived. However, a friendly co-op that ran the only restaurant and café inside the park, and that served excellent local food, was replaced by a cafeteria run by a highway franchise chain.

More seriously, cheap materials bought at exorbitant prices were used for seating throughout Pompeii's splendid ancient

Above, left: **In earlier centuries, fine frescos like *Theseus the Liberator*** were removed for display in royal collections. This shows the Minotaur lying dead at the feet of the hero Theseus, who has just freed the grateful children of Athens. Typifying the Romans' fondness for Greek culture, the scene echoes a fourth century B.C.E. Greek original. When the wall painting, found in the House of Gavius Rufus at Herculaneum, was removed, it was given a concrete backing, which damaged the picture. Although archeologists criticized this practice, removing the frescos saved them from vandalism and bleaching in the sun and rain.
National Archaeological

Above, right: **Here is the same fresco of *Theseus the Liberator*** after a recent restoration at the Conservation and Restoration Laboratory of the National Archaeological Museum in Naples. The concrete backing was removed and the fresco was remounted on a lightweight aluminum panel and cleaned, restoring its original colors.

Greek-style theater to allow commercial evening events. In July 2011, prosecutors seized examples of all materials for an analysis of their real value. Inside the city walls, an ancient road with original paving stones was cemented over. The newest park plan is still evolving, with international consultation and funding from, among other sources, the European Union.

In a formal inquiry in 2010, the national Corte dei Conti (General Accounting Office) assailed the emergency declaration as "unjustifiable." The "life of the heritage" had not been protected, said its report, while the emergency declaration was utilized to justify over-payment for materials, inappropriate restorations, and needless high-tech "entertainment archeology." Judicial inquiries over alleged crony contracting and other serious misdeeds followed, and in 2011 the special commissioner was removed. Site management returned to a Cultural

Heritage Ministry archeologist who must also administer the many dauntingly complex sites throughout the entire Naples area as well as Pompeii. The Cultural Heritage Ministry's budget is shrinking drastically each year, and a freeze on hiring diminishes its senior staff pool from which Pompeii's administrators are drawn. At Pompeii, similar staff reductions mean that the 279 custodians of 15 years ago were only 197 in 2012, even as fragile Pompeii continues to draw between 2.1 and 2.6 million tourists every year.

Today the Cultural Ministry promises new funding that, according to the minister, will allow hiring of personnel and better maintenance. European Union funds are also being sought. The Pompeii administrators say they need 14 archeologists and as many architects and skilled technicians. The site is owned by the national government, but Italy spends only 0.1 percent of its GNP on its cultural heritage. As elsewhere in southern Europe, the economic crisis has brought cut-backs, and the 2.3 billion euros ($2.96 billion) from Italy's 2001 budget for culture shrank to 1.4 billion euros ($1.8 billion) in 2012.

To compensate, efforts are being made to rent the name Pompeii as a brand to international commercial sponsors, as has already happened at the Coliseum in Rome, where a shoe manufacturer received a 15-year exclusive on the commercial use of the Coliseum image in exchange for about $37 million toward its maintenance. At Pompeii, another fundraising effort is the rental of artifacts to foreign museums, from frescos to bronze frying pans.

From 2000 until 2009, Pompeii was run by the equivalent of co-chairs: an archeologist in the employ of the Cultural

Ministry teamed with a professional city manager with experience in cultural heritage management. This system should be reinstated. But the drastic budget cuts at the Ministry in Rome mean that no new personnel with up-to-date training in either archeology or administration—and both skills are essential—are being hired. In addition, because corruption is endemic, transparent bidding procedures are essential.

Advances in Archeology and Conservation

The archeological riches of the Gulf of Naples area continue to attract and excite archeologists from around the world. In cooperation with the Soprintendenza Archeologica di Napoli e Pompei, universities from some 40 nations currently have projects here. Some restudy old excavations. A few are making test borings in roads and previously excavated buildings to explore the pre-Roman town.

New, less-invasive techniques are already available, such as ground-penetrating radar, which permits mapping a buried site without excavating. Conservation techniques improve, but are expensive. One innovative system allows the recomposition of fresco paintings—often found shattered into miniscule fragments—by computerized calculations of fragment widths.

Although suggestions have been made for over a century that Pompeii be internationalized, that is unlikely, given century-old Italian legislation that places all cultural heritage sites under exclusive state ownership. However, Pompeii's sister-in-distress, Herculaneum, has had significant expert help from foreign archeologists thanks to a generous grant

from the Packard Humanities Institute of California working with the Italian State Soprintendenza and with the British School at Rome. Italians consider the Herculaneum Conservation Project a model of cooperation.

One third of the walled city of Pompeii remains underground, and archeologists are firmly determined that it should remain buried to protect it for future generations and future less-invasive technologies. The goal is to devote available income to maintenance, which includes increasing the number of custodians, skilled artisans, and trained archeologists on the site.

The former tradition of resident skilled artisans for common repairs could and should be revived. Repairs require specific training in the use of low-tech materials, including wood. For instance, had the roof of the House of the Gladiators been made of wood rather than modern cement, it is unlikely that it would have collapsed.

Pompeii park management issues tickets to encourage tourists to visit the Greek-influenced resort town of Herculaneum, the recently excavated (1960s) maritime villa of Oplontis, important villas at Stabiae, and the delightful small teaching

This charred loaf of bread is on view along with an iron sickle in the small museum at Boscoreale near Pompeii. This shape of bread roll can still be found in Roman bakeries today.
Photo by David Willey

Right: **Black and white mosaic floors** were typical in luxurious Pompeian interiors. If not protected and maintained, the exposed floors disintegrate from weathering and the pounding of millions of footsteps. Tourists sometimes snatch up mosaic bits for souvenirs. Guilt-ridden, some then return the pieces by mail, but no one knows where they originally lay.
Photo by Joel Katz

museum and Roman farm at Boscoreale. The goal is to keep these worthwhile sites financially viable as well as to reduce the pressure on Pompeii. And in fact, the number of visitors to Oplontis and Boscoreale has increased. But Pompeii is unique in the world and will always be the primary attraction.

Following are some of the many archeological projects in and around Pompeii today:

● Archeologist John Dobbins of the University of Virginia is at work in the Forum. The Pompeii Forum Project has reconstructed a virtual version of the large and imposing Imperial Cult Building dedicated to the Emperor Vespasian, who sent Pompeii significant contributions for rebuilding after the earthquake of 68 C.E.

● Steven Ellis of the University of

Cincinnati directs the Pompeii Archaeological Research Project in the neighborhood near one city gate, the Porta Stabia. An important discovery in this largely overlooked working-class neighborhood was evidence of a cottage industry of curing salted fish in underground vats.

● The Oplontis Project at Torre Annunziata is co-directed by John R. Clarke and Michael L. Thomas of the University of Texas at Austin. In coordination with the *Soprintendenza* of Pompeii, the project is conducting a systematic, multidisciplinary study of the luxurious and sprawling so-called Villa of Poppaea.

● Stabiae has several well-preserved luxurious ancient villas built on cliffs overlooking the sea. The Restoring Ancient Stabiae Foundation is working

Above: **The eruption of 79 C.E.** shoved the shoreline below Pompeii forward by perhaps a quarter-mile. Here, just below the city walls of Pompeii at its point closest to the sea, was the dock of a canal connecting either to the sea or to the Sarno River, but now entirely filled in. The existence of the dock is demonstrated by the square stone moorings in a file along the dockside. The umbrella pines in the distance are among the glories of the Italian coastal landscape.
Photo by David Willey

Above: **Ironically, the gate here reads "Pompeii Lives."** But as archeologists know, to dig is to destroy, for time and weather will always take their toll. After the collapse of the House of the Gladiators in 2010, this and many other streets at Pompeii were closed to visitors. Some walls bordering streets have recently been shored up by scaffolding.

Photo David Willey

to link them in a single archeological park. Two villas are now protected by innovative flexible roofing and ultraviolet-resistant glass.

● The villa at Somma Vesuviana is thought to have belonged to the family of the Emperor Augustus. Excavation here is under the aegis of Tokyo University, together with the Pompeii archeological authorities.

● The Villa dei Papyri at Herculaneum yielded almost 1,000 carbonized Greek scrolls preserved in volcanic mud that solidified into rock. It is the only surviving ancient library. The international classicists associated with the Philodemus Project are working at the national library in Naples to analyze the miniscule fragments of charred scrolls and to restudy the sometimes scrambled 18th-century copies of them. Scientists hope that powerful X-ray

equipment will permit digital scanning rather than the physical unrolling of the crumbling scrolls.

Where to Learn More

BOOKS

Mary Beard. *The Fires of Vesuvius.* Cambridge, Mass.: Harvard University Press, 2008.

Edward Bulwer-Lytton. *The Last Days of Pompeii* [1834]. Rockville, Md.: Wildside Press, 2007, fiction.

Robert Harris. *Pompeii.* New York: Random House, 2003, fiction.

Judith Harris. *Pompeii Awakened: A Story of Rediscovery.* New York and London: I. B. Tauris, 2007.

Roger Ling. *Pompeii: History, Life and Afterlife.* Stroud, England: Tempus Publishing, Ltd., 2005.

Andrew Wallace-Hadrill. *Herculaneum*. London: Frances Lincoln, 2011.

VIDEOS AND FILM

The Last Days of Pompeii (1926). Directors Carmine Gallone, Amleto Palermi. Epochal Italian silent film based on the Bulwer-Lytton novel.

The Last Days of Pompeii (1935). RKO. Starring Preston Foster and Basil Rathbone. A historic remake of the Gallone-Palermi film.

Pompeii (forthcoming). Director Paul W.S. Anderson.

WEBSITES

Google Street View for a "walk" about the ruins of Pompeii:
http://google-mapping.blogspot.it/2009/12/visita-pompei-scavi-con-google-street.html

For the Naples Archaeological Museum treasures, see the home page in English with image gallery:
http://museoarcheologiconazionale.campaniabeniculturali.it/thematic-views?set_language=en

On the Herculaneum Project:
http://www.bsr.ac.uk/research/archaeology/ongoing-projects/herculaneum/herculaneum-conservation-project

On the Philodemus Project for study and restoration of the precious Herculaneum papyri:
http://www.classics.ucla.edu/index.php/philodemus

World Monument Fund Symposium of 2003:
Conservation in the Shadow of Vesuvius: A Review of Best Practices
www.wmf.org/project/ancient-pompeii

Tiny glass paste tiles (tesserae) were used to create a vividly colored mosaic panel inserted into a wall of the outdoor dining courtyard of the House of Neptune and Amphitrite at Herculaneum, Pompeii's neighboring town. The panel illustrates the taste for elegance of the Roman elite, whose villas overlooked the Bay of Naples in the first century C.E. Amphitrite was the wife of the sea god Neptune.
Public domain

On the Alexander Mosaic from Pompeii, now in the Naples Archaeological Museum: http://news.discovery.com/history/how-the-alexander-mosaic-was-used.html

For information on a research project into food and drink at Pompeii: http://www.pompeii-food-and-drink.org/

How to Get Involved

Surprisingly, there are no nonprofit support groups for Pompeii. But see: The Friends of Herculaneum Society, http://www.herculaneum.ox.ac.uk/?q=Hom

VISITING NAPLES AND POMPEII

The treasures unearthed at Pompeii, from the finest frescos and statues to frying pans, are in the National Archeological Museum in Naples, not at the ruins. Bronze and marble statues and brightly colored mosaics from Herculaneum are there as well. The Villa of the Mysteries on the outskirts of Pompeii has a famous fresco cycle on the initiation of young girls to life as married women. The recently excavated villa at Oplontis has the most vivid frescos. The worst months to visit are July and August, which bring overcrowding and ferocious heat. The best times are September–October and May–June. In January, snow may cap Mount Vesuvius, but Pompeii can be wonderfully sunny and uncrowded, if chilly.

In the 18th century, the kings of Naples decreed that the Crown owned all excavated artifacts. Many of the precious objects found at Pompeii were kept in the royal palace at Portici at the foot of Mount Vesuvius. Later these treasures were removed to the archeological museum in Naples, where they can be seen today. This bronze Tripod with Satyrs from the House of Julia Felix, a wealthy businesswoman, exemplifies the luxury objects found at Pompeii. With their left hands the sinuous, ithyphallic satyrs are warding away evil while balancing a bowl on their heads. The tripod occupied the center of a shrine room whose other cult statuettes depicted the Egyptian deities Isis, Osiris, and Anubis.
Museo Archeologico Nazionale di Napoli

Alto Orinoco-Casiquiare Biosphere Reserve, Venezuela, and Yanomami Territory, Brazil

National Reserves and the Yanomami People in the Amazonian Rainforest

Fiona Watson and Joanna Eede

Survival International, London

We are children of the land, we are children of the forest.

—Davi Kopenawa Yanomami, shaman and spokesperson for the Yanomami people

Deep in southern Venezuela lies an important biosphere reserve known as Alto Orinoco–Casiquiare. It is a vast area of dense tropical rainforest, forested lowland, and sandstone table-mountains known as tepui along the reaches of the Upper Orinoco River in Amazonas state.

The Venezuelan president declared the area a Biosphere Reserve in 1991. In the same year, the European Union declared it to be one of the most valuable ecosystems in the world. It became a UNESCO biosphere reserve in 1992 in order to secure the ancestral homelands of the Yanomami and Ye'kuana tribes.

The Alto Orinoco-Casiquiare is the largest biosphere reserve in the tropics. It contains two previously recognized national parks: Duida-Marahuaca and Serranía La Neblina. At the same time that the biosphere was created, Parima-Tapirapecó National Park, where most of the indigenous people live, was included in the biosphere. The indigenous population is estimated at 21,000 people, of which 16,000 are Yanomami and 5,000 are Ye'kuana.

"These sacred places, the high mountains, are the homes of the spirits. We call them hutu papa."

—Davi Kopenawa Yanomami

The Alto Orinoco-Casiquiare is a place of contrasts. The altitude in the reserve ranges from near zero on the plateau of Casiquiare canal to the 9,800-foot Pico de la Neblina. The peak is part of the Sierra de la Neblina, a relatively isolated sandstone massif. The reserve is thick with life. Animal species include the golden-mantled tamarin, jaguar, and white-lipped peccary; snakes include the emerald tree boa, fer-de-lance, coral snake, and palm-pit vipers; birds include crestless curassows and tufted toucanets.

For centuries, the remoteness of the Yanomami's terrain made journeys along the broad rivers, rapids, and waterfalls impossible for outsiders. As a result, the Yanomami in both Venezuela and Brazil

Left: **Face of man in trance.**
Claudia Andujar / Survival International

were virtually isolated from the world until the 1940s. Even today, not all Yanomami communities have been contacted. Brazilian Yanomami have seen uncontacted Yanomami, whom they call *Moxi hatëtëma thëpë* (the people who tie up the foreskin with two strings), in their territory.

The Yanomami and Ye'Kuana

The Yanomami people are one of the largest relatively isolated tribes in South America. Their ancestors probably migrated across the Bering Strait between Asia and America, perhaps as early as 15,000 or 16,000 years ago, making their way slowly down the continent to South America. The Yanomami's Amazonian territory spans 23.7 million acres in Brazil and 20.3 million acres in the Alto Orinoco-Casiquiare, which combined makes it the largest forested indigenous territory in the world, equivalent in size to Missouri or Cambodia. The Yanomami, however, have never recognized the border between Brazil and Venezuela. To them, their homeland is one ancestral territory.

Yanomami women traditionally wear bunches of leaves or flowers in their pierced ears, and cotton bands around their upper arms. They also decorate themselves with scented leaves and flowers, and pierce their lower lips and noses with sharpened sticks.

In Brazil, the Yanomami first came into sustained contact with outsiders in the 1940s, when the government sent teams to establish the border with Venezuela. In the Venezuelan territory, some of the first contacts also occurred with Salesian missionaries in the 1940s, when the Venezuelan government gave them responsibility for schools for indigenous peoples in Amazonas state. Today there are approximately 18,000 Yanomami and 500 Ye'kuana in Brazil.

Yanomami paint motifs on their faces using black dye from the genipapo tree and scarlet dye from the urucum shrub. Urucum is also rubbed onto the forehead of a hunter and his dogs to ensure good fortune in a hunt.

Previous pages: **The Alto-Orinoco Casiquiare Biosphere Reserve.**
Fiona Watson / Survival International

Above: **Pico de la Neblina.**

Top: **Yanomami woman**.
Fiona Watson / Survival International

Above: **Yanomami boy with piercings**.
Victor Engelbert / Survival International

The Ye'kuana are river people, famous for their boat building and basket weaving skills. They traditionally lived in communal houses with cone-shaped roofs, but today most have been replaced by *criollo* (settler)-style houses constructed from mud bricks with tin roofs. The Ye'kuana practice polygyny; a man may have two or more wives. They cultivate gardens where they grow manioc, tobacco, cotton, and medicinal plants. They also hunt and fish.

Communal Life / Shabono

Dependent on each other for survival in remote environments, many tribal peoples, including the Yanomami, live in complex communities where the solidarity of the group is of utmost importance. The Yanomami believe they are descendants of the creator god *Omame*, who also created the trees, rivers, and mountains.

Yanomami live in communal homes called *shabonos* or *yanos*. These can be open or closed. Open *shabonos* have a central area that is open to the sky where children play and ceremonial events take place. Families occupy individual hearths around the central plaza. It is a village under one roof. From the clearing that surrounds the *shabono*, narrow paths lead out into the forest in all directions.

The Yanomami are shifting cultivators. *Shabonos* are moved to rotate the

gardens, rest the earth, and open up new gardens. In some regions, increased contact with outsiders such as health workers and state officials has resulted in more sedentary communities. This has resulted in the depletion of nearby natural resources and game.

Up to 400 people can live in a *shabono* or *yano*, although most house 50 to 200 people. Each village is autonomous, but communities constantly interact with each other. Runners are sent through the forest with invitations to festivities that can last for days, when vast quantities

of banana soup, plantain, smoked meat, manioc beer, and manioc bread are enjoyed. Feasts are an important way of celebrating marriages, cementing alliances with neighboring communities, and of exchanging goods. One of the most celebrated of Yanomami festivals is the peach-palm festival when the ripe fruit is collected; another is *reahu*, a funeral rite.

The Yanomami believe strongly in equality and do not recognize any chiefs. Decisions are made by consensus, frequently after long debates where everybody has a say. As in any society, there are conflicts.

A Yanomami communal home or *shabono*.

Sometimes these are resolved when communities split up and form separate groups. Inter-community disputes are usually caused by sexual jealousies or accusations of sorcery. Rivals may beat each other's chests, or perform ritualized duelling with sticks. This rarely results in serious injury.

Unfortunately, the Yanomami have been sensationally characterized by one anthropologist as the "fierce people." This is disputed by other anthropologists. They are not especially violent, either amongst themselves or towards outsiders. Often tensions are reduced by humor and joking. In the last 30 years, many more Yanomami have died from diseases introduced by outsiders and in violent encounters with gold miners than from internal conflicts. Outsiders who have lived with the Yanomami have been struck by their sense of humor, the richness of their shamanism, and how well they live, with ample time for leisure and socializing.

Shunning or ostracizing an offending individual is the method usually chosen to deal with irresponsible behavior. There is a high degree of tolerance for those with mental health problems, who are considered as much a part of the community as any other member.

Values and social mechanisms have evolved over time and favor the group over the individual. As a result, sharing is fundamental to Yanomami life—personal property is very limited—and all food is shared around the hearth. The greatest transgression in Yanomami society is stinginess. As a symbol of the willingness to share, hunters never carry their own game back to the *shabono*. They also believe that if a hunter eats his own game, he will become ill. Land is collectively held and the community has a joint responsibility to safeguard it.

At night in the *shabono*, hammocks are slung around the fires. Theirs is an oral

Above left: **Woman preparing manioc**.
Victor Engelbert / Survival International

Left: **Yanomami men in hammocks, eating**.
Victor Engelbert / Survival International

Most mothers carry children on their hips in a sling for the best part of two years.

A Yanomami child's education is a continuous process of observation and practice. Through watching and imitating the adults, children discover what it means to be a member of the tribe. From the age of 5, boys start to accompany their fathers on hunting trips. They learn to shin up trees by tying their feet together with liana vines for extra grip and practice hunting small birds with bows and arrows. Girls help their mothers gather fruit and vegetables from the gardens.

Food, Medicine, and Knowledge of the Forest

"We know our Yanomami land well. We know the streams and the rapids, the paths of the peccary, the call of the tapir, and the song of the toucan. We call it *Urihi*—our place, our land—and we know that it is beautiful."

—Davi Kopenawa Yanomami

Yanomami group in the forest.

Fiona Watson / Survival International

tradition, rich in tales, creation myths, and memories that recall mythical creatures and heroes. Respect for the natural world permeates their stories. This not only helps to educate Yanomami children about the history of their people, but it also imparts concepts of responsibility and balance.

A form of unleavened bread made from manioc is a staple of the Yanomami diet. Manioc was developed by South American Indians and has become an extremely important world food.

Women give birth to their children in the forests surrounding their community. They go into the forest accompanied by other women, who help them through labor.

The Yanomami have a holistic view of nature and see man as part of, not separate from, the environment. Many areas that are richest in biodiversity, such as the Amazon, remain so due to the care of the people who have lived in them for thousands of years. To the Yanomami, the rainforest is the bedrock of their lives: the provider of food and shelter and, importantly, the inheritance of their children. Their way of life is inextricably linked to their forest home, *Urihi*. "We know that it is alive, that it has a long breath of life, much longer than ours," they say.

For thousands of years, the Yanomami have lived in intimate harmony with the forest. "It is part of us, the blood in our veins." They have always treated *Urihi* with great respect and care, knowing that to take more than is needed, or to degrade the forest in any way, is not only self-defeating, but will threaten their children's future. Such continuous immersion in, and observation of, nature has resulted not only in a profound attunement with the subtle cues of nature, but also in an encyclopedic knowledge of animals and plants.

The Yanomami utilize approximately 500 species of rainforest plants for food, building materials, hunting poisons, and medicines. Their *shabonos* are made from hardwood poles lashed together with liana vines and covered with palm frond thatch. Men make longbows from canes and arrowheads from palm wood, while women make necklaces from fruit seeds and silk-grass thread. Women seduce men with the perfume from plants such as water willow. They weave mats and baskets from the fibers of the piassava palm tree.

Their pharmacopeia is vital for Yanomami nutrition and health. The bark of the copal tree is applied to eye infections, the juice of cat's claw vine is used to treat diarrhea, and crushed aromatic leaves are inhaled to alleviate colds and nausea. The poison curare, which Yanomami hunters have long used on the tips of arrows to paralyze prey, has been appropriated by Western medicine as a muscle relaxant. The Yanomami use various wild forest plants, mostly lianas, to make fish poison. Bundles of vines are pounded in the water, releasing the poison and stunning the fish, which then rise to the surface. The fish are scooped up in baskets and grilled in leaf parcels over a fire. Because the poison breaks down quickly, it does not pollute the rivers.

The Yanomami diet consists of game such as tapir and peccary, together with nuts, fruit, crustaceans, honey, caterpillars, fish, frogs, and land crabs, which they dig from their burrows at the foot of trees. They also eat manioc, a starchy tuber from which they make bread. Women tend Yanomami gardens, which can contain up to 60 crops, including manioc, peach palms, papaya trees, banana, plantains, sugarcane, maize, and sweet potato. They also cultivate tobacco. Garden produce accounts for approximately 80 percent of the Yanomami diet. They generally move every few years in order to give the plot back to the forest and open up a new area for cultivation.

Carrying longbows up to 6 feet, Yanomami men file into the forest. Only the men can hunt, which is considered a highly prestigious and sophisticated skill. Hunters read animal tracks and can recognize the sounds of almost all animals and birds, which they mimic in order to attract them. Male prestige rests on hunting ability.

Dancing with the Spirits

The spirit world is a fundamental part of Yanomami life. Every creature, rock, tree, and mountain is present in the spirit world. They also believe there is little distinction between the living and spirit worlds, and that every Yanomami has a double in the animal world with which they are joined until death.

"It comes from the deepest part and reaches to a future we cannot imagine," say the Yanomami about the spiritual dimension to life. Their shamans communicate with the natural world and its spirits not only for the benefit of his community but also for humanity as

Yanomami hunters in forest.
Raymond Depardon / Palmeraie
et désert

a whole. Through dreams and trances, shamans transcend the physical confines of their bodies and the limits of human consciousness to commune with spirits (*xapiripë*).

In order to enter a dream state, Yanomami shamans inhale *yakoana* or *yopo* powder extracted from the bark resin of the virola tree. The powder is inhaled through a long tube called a *horoma*, traditionally created from the hollowed stem of a palm tree. "This is how we make the spirits dance," says Davi Kopenawa Yanomami. Guided by spirits and the wisdom of their ancestors, Yanomami shamans *(xapiripë thëpë)* are able to command thunderstorms and caution the winds. They prevent the sky from falling down, ensure hunting successes, and put to flight hostile spirits known as *yai* that crawl into human bodies.

"The *xapiripë* descend to us on threads as fine as a spider's web. They are beautiful, painted with bright colors and *urucum* (annatto). Their armlets are decorated

with macaw and parrot feathers. There are different songs: the song of the macaw, of the parrot, of the tapir, of the tortoise, and of the eagle. The *xapiripë* have danced for shamans since the very beginning of time, and they continue to dance today. Their heads are covered with white hawk down, and they wear black bands made of monkey tails and turquoise cotinga feathers in their ears. They dance in a circle, unhurriedly," says Davi Kopenawa Yanomami.

One of the main functions of the Yanomami shaman is to cure the sick. Diagnosing and detecting diseases takes years of shamanistic experience. Over time, they have developed complex, holistic health systems that combine spiritual healing with herbal remedies. In general, every ailment has its cure, except for diseases that have been brought in by outsiders to which the Yanomami have little immunity. "Our wisdom is different. Our knowledge is a different knowledge. It is the wisdom of the shamanic spirits, which is very important for the survival of humanity," says Davi Kopenawa Yanomami.

By communing with and controlling *xapiripë,* Yanomami shamans believe that they are not only protecting their own community but are also looking after the rest of the world. "Our shamans know that our planet is changing," says Davi Kopenawa Yanomami. "We know the health of the Amazon. We know that it is dangerous to abuse nature, and that when you destroy the rainforest, you cut the arteries of the future and the world's force just ebbs away."

The Crisis

"They built dusty roads, cut the skin of the earth with machines, and poisoned the rivers with mercury."

—Davi Kopenawa Yanomami

In Venezuela, the government launched its Conquista del Sur (Conquest of the South) program in 1969, which brought with it roads, towns, and an influx of criollos (non-indigenous settlers) and put pressure on Indians and on the land. In the early 1970s, the Brazilian government built a stretch of the Perimetral Norte (Northern Perimeter Highway), part of Brazil's National Integration Plan, through part of Yanomami territory. As a result, two villages were wiped out from diseases to which the residents had no immunity. The road was later abandoned and taken over by cattle ranchers and colonists, which has led to deforestation and colonization of the southeastern part of Yanomami territory.

"We are removed from our lands so that governments and corporations can carry out logging and road building and the mining that unearths gold and diamonds. We are on top of the government's riches."

—Davi Kopenawa Yanomami

Above: **Head with feathers** seen from behind.
Claudia Andujar / Survival International

Below: **Man in a dream state**.
Claudia Andujar / Survival International

Right page, top: **A road through Yanomami territory stretches to the horizon**.
Credit: Bruce Albert / Survival International

Right page, middle: **Yanomami in newly cut road**.
Bruce Albert / Survival International

Right page, bottom: **Gold mining equipment**.
Fiona Watson / Survival International

In recent decades, the mineral-rich Amazonian territory of the Yanomami has been exploited for gold and minerals, farming, logging, military bases, and other development. Yanomami territory is rich in minerals such as gold and cassiterite. During the 20th century, for the first time in their long history of living in and stewarding their rainforest, the Yanomami and Ye'kuana witnessed the horrific destruction of their environment and the demise of their peoples.

The Creation of Yanomami Reserves

During the 1980s, approximately 40,000 Brazilian gold miners (garimpeiros) working illegally invaded Yanomami land. They opened clandestine airstrips, killed Yanomami and exposed them to potentially fatal diseases such as malaria, measles, and flu. With the garimpeiros came machinery, shotguns, alcohol, and prostitution. The miners' high-pressure hoses destroyed the riverbanks. The sound of their planes, generators, and guns scared away the birds and mammals on which the Yanomami depend. Their use of mercury destroyed aquatic life, poisoned fish, and caused birth defects, and could take years to filter out of the ecosystems. Pools of stagnant water created through gold mining became breeding areas for malarial mosquitoes. The consequences of the sudden arrival of the garimpeiros were catastrophic. In seven years, 20 percent of the Yanomami population in the Brazilian part of the territory died from imported diseases. The Yanomami refer to these epidemics as xawara. By 1989, 90 percent of Yanomami were suffering from malaria.

In Venezuela, responsibility for protecting the biosphere lies with the Ministry of the Environment. Both the Venezuelan

National Guard and military have posts in the border region but have failed to expel the gold miners. Some have been accused of corruption and colluding with the miners.

In July 1993, 16 Yanomami, mainly old people and children, were massacred by Brazilian *garimpeiros* in the village of Haximu on the Venezuelan-Brazilian border. In 1996, in a landmark ruling, a Brazilian court convicted five gold miners of genocide. Today, more than 1,000 gold miners are still working illegally on Yanomami land. Rates of malaria among the Brazilian Yanomami are down, but the Venezuelan Yanomami are severely affected in some areas because of difficulty in accessing the highlands where they live and the resulting lack of medical care.

From the late 1970s, concerned activists and anthropologists in Venezuela lobbied for protection of Yanomami land with the support of Survival International. This resulted in the creation of the Alto Casiquiare-Orinoco biosphere reserve and the Parima-Tapirapecó National Park within the biosphere in 1991. Special provisions recognized the Yanomami's right to occupy the land and use its natural resources. In 1992, after a long international campaign led by Davi Kopenawa Yanomami, Survival International and the CCPY (Pro Yanomami Commission), Yanomami land in Brazil was demarcated and the miners expelled from the newly created reserve. Today, gold mining continues to have adverse consequences on the natural environment and the Yanomami.

"Our blood is flowing, we are hungry and we are ill. The illnesses have never gone away. The whites that brought them here have left them here. We are still dying."

Roman Catholic and evangelical missionaries are active on both sides of the Venezuelan-Brazilian border. In both countries, the Catholic Church supports Yanomami land rights. Consolata missionaries have had a base inside Yanomami territory in Brazil since 1965. They conduct a school and provide health care. The Salesians in Venezuela operate schools in three Yanomami communities. The New Tribes Mission, a fundamentalist evangelical missionary organization, also works among the Yanomami in both countries. Their aim to convert indigenous peoples to Christianity is controversial and has had limited success. In 2005, the president of Venezuela expelled them from the area.

Some communities exchange goods with neighboring tribes, but since the region is remote, it is difficult and expensive to sell produce. Others occasionally sell artifacts such as baskets, but tourism is forbidden in the reserves. Anthropologists, botanists, ecologists, doctors, and non-governmental organizations work with the Yanomami in the region and many have long advocated for Yanomami rights.

Action Now: Health, Land Rights, and Self-Determination

When living on their own land and employing the techniques and values they have honed over generations, tribal peoples are typically healthy, self-sufficient, and happy. "The Yanomami don't die of hunger, they only die of disease. They have everything that they need to survive when there are no miners. We know what is best for our people," says Davi Kopenawa Yanomami.

But the Yanomami cannot cure imported diseases such as malaria. They rely on Western medicine to treat them. The Brazilian and Venezuelan governments, missionaries, and non-governmental organizations have built health clinics in the reserves where medical staff dispense medicines. In Brazil, non-governmental organizations have trained Yanomami health workers. The challenges of working in such a vast, remote area are great. Many communities have only sporadic access to health care, and some have no access at all. In Brazil, there have been attempts to politicize health care by appointing party members to head the Yanomami health district. Health care has also been undermined by corruption; government officials have stolen large sums of money from the health program. Survival International helped fund healthcare together with the Yanomami in Venezuela in 1984 and in Brazil in the 1990s.

Neither Brazil nor Venezuela recognizes the Yanomami's right to collective land ownership, even though both have ratified the International Labour Organization's Convention 169 on tribal and indigenous peoples, which asserts

© Survival

© Steve Cox/Survival

this fundamental right. In Brazil, the federal government owns indigenous lands, and the constitution recognizes indigenous peoples' right to occupy and use it exclusively. Although the Venezuelan constitution does proclaim indigenous peoples' collective property rights, few titles have been recognized. The biosphere and national parks offer some legal protection—the Yanomami and Ye'kuana have usufruct rights—and colonization and resource extraction by outsiders is forbidden.

Collective title is the most secure way to protect indigenous land. At the moment, since the Yanomami do not own their land, the territories can be altered or shrunk by presidential decree. The challenge now is for the Yanomami to secure collective title to their territory and to be recognized as the legal owners. In Brazil, the government's Indian affairs department,

FUNAI, is responsible for protecting Yanomami territory. But it does not have enough funding or people on the ground to monitor invasions. The Brazilian federal police are often slow to remove intruders. The military, which has three bases there, rarely acts to stop invasions.

The Yanomami and Ye'kuana are increasingly active in the defense of their land and their rights. They interact with a wide range of state bodies and attend meetings outside their reserves. They hold demonstrations and petition the authorities to take action. They have set up their own indigenous organizations. Yanomami spokesmen have travelled abroad to press for their rights and to raise money to fund their own projects.

Until 1988, the Yanomami of Brazil were denied full citizenship. They are still considered legal minors by the courts. In

A Yanomami woman holding her child with river in background.
© *Steve Cox / Survival*

1992, after a long international campaign led by Davi Kopenawa Yanomami, Survival International, and the Pro Yanomami Commission (a Brazilian non-governmental organization), Yanomami land in Brazil was recognized. In 2004, Yanomami from 11 regions met in Brazil to form their own organization, Hutukara, meaning "the part of the sky from which the earth was born," to defend their rights and run their own projects. As a result of increasing contact with outsiders, the Yanomami and the Pro Yanomami Commission created a Yanomami education project. One of its principal aims is to raise awareness among the Yanomami of their rights. Yanomami are trained to teach reading, writing, and mathematics in their communities. Others have been trained as health workers by *Urihi,* a non-governmental organization that provided health care.

Venezuela's constitution of 1999 guarantees indigenous peoples the right to collective ownership of their lands, but the land rights of the Yanomami and the Ye'kuana have still not been formally recognized. The Yanomami in Venezuela established an organization called Horonami Organización Yanomami in 2011. The solution to the problems of the Yanomami, and all tribal peoples, is relatively simple. It lies in the recognition of two basic rights: the right to land and the right to self-determination.

Despite recent positive developments, the Yanomami and all Amazonian Indians are still vulnerable. They need to be treated as equals and consulted about decisions that affect them. They need respect from the world for their way of life, beliefs, and rituals. They want others to understand that their lack of material goods or formal education does not signify that they are backward, "Stone Age," or primitive. "We know how to defend nature. We have never lost that knowledge," they say. Crucially, the Yanomami and Ye'kuana—and all tribal peoples—have the right to live the lives they choose, now and in the future, not the lives other people think they should live. "It is not that the Yanomami do not want progress. We want to be able to choose and not have change thrust upon us. We want progress without destruction," says Davi Kopenawa Yanomami.

"I thank all of you who are very far away and who don't know my people or my forest. I am sending this message to boys and girls there, everyone. Continue with the campaign, continue fighting and defending the Yanomami people. ... The Earth demands a greater respect. If we hurt nature, we also hurt ourselves. Our way of thinking is based on the land. Our interest is in preserving the earth. Where will we go when we have destroyed our world? When the planet is silent, how will we learn?"

—Davi Kopenawa Yanomami

Where to Learn More

SURVIVAL INTERNATIONAL

Survival International, www.survivalinternational.org, is the only organization working for tribal peoples' rights worldwide that does not accept government funding. We help tribal peoples protect their lives, lands, and human rights. Our vision is to foster an understanding of, and respect for, tribal peoples and the choices they make about their futures, and for a world where tribal peoples are free to live on their own lands, safe from violence, oppression, and exploitation.

YOU CAN HELP TRIBAL PEOPLES BY:

Giving. We depend almost entirely on thousands of small donations. This gives us great independence. It ensures we never adjust our message or work to suit donors.

Keeping up with news and events through our monthly e-news, blogs, press releases, features, and daily reports.

Following us on Facebook. The number of people who see our material is an indication of our strength.

Writing to those in power. Our letter campaigns generate thousands of letters and e-mails. Every voice counts. Write to the Presidents of Brazil and Venezuela:

President Dilma Vana Rousseff, Gabinete do Presidente. Palácio do Planalto, Praça dos Três Poderes, Brasília, DF 70150-900, Brazil.

President Hugo Rafael Chávez Frías, Palacio de Miraflores, Carmelitas, Caracas 1010, Venezuela.

Signing our petitions. We present them to governments and corporations with hundreds of thousands of signatures. This can shame them into action. It can also attract media attention in favor of justice for tribal peoples.

WEBSITES

Hutukara:
http://hutukara.org/

Instituto Socioambiental (Brazilian NGO working with Yanomami on education and land protection projects):
www.socioambiental.org

BOOKS

Much has been written on the Yanomami. The following is a selection of the more accessible literature.

Bruce Albert. "Gold Miners and the Yanomami Indians in the Brazilian Amazon: The Hashimu massacre." In Johnston, B. R., ed. *Who Pays the Price? The Sociocultural Context of Environmental Crisis.* Washington, D.C.: Island Press, 1994, pp. 47–55.

Claudia Andujar. *Marcados.* São Paulo, Brazil: Cosac Naify, 2009.

D. Berwick. *Savages: The Life and Killing of the Yanomami.* London: Hodder and Stoughton, 1992.

Robert and Albert Bruce Borofsky. *Yanomami: The Fierce Controversy and What We Can Learn from It.* Berkeley, Calif.: University of California Press, 2005.

K. Good with D. Chanoff. *Into the Heart: One Man's Pursuit of Love and Knowledge Among the Yanomama.* New York: Simon and Schuster, 1991.

J. Lizot. *Tales of the Yanomami: Daily Life in the Venezuelan Forest.* New York: Cambridge University Press, 1985.

Davi Kopenawa and Bruce Albert. *The Falling Sky: Words of a Yanomami Shaman.* Cambridge, Mass.: Harvard University Press, November 2013.

Gordon MacMillan. *At the End of the Rainbow? Gold, Land, and People in the Brazilian Amazon.* New York: Columbia University Press, 1995.

William Milliken and Bruce Albert with Gale Goodwin Gomez. *Yanomami, A Forest People.* London: The Royal Botanic Gardens, 1999.

A. R. Ramos. *Sanuma Memories: Yanomami Ethnography in Times of Crisis.* Madison, Wis.: University of Wisconsin Press, 1995.

Jan Rocha. *Murder in the Rainforest: The Yanomami, the Gold Miners and the Amazon.* London: Latin America Bureau, 1999.

Patrick Tierney. *Darkness in El Dorado: How Scientists and Journalists Devastated the Amazon.* New York: W. W. Norton, 2000.

Survival International. *Disinherited: The Indians of Brazil.* London, 2000.

VIDEOS AND FILMS

David contra Golias: Brasil Caim (1993). Director Aurélio Michiles. Producer Cedi/PIB.

La maison et la foret (1993). Director Volkmar Ziegler. Producers Volkmar Ziegler, Pierrette Birraux.

Povo da Lua, Povo do Sangue: Yanomami (1983). Director Marcelo Tassara.

Secrets of the Tribe (2011). Director José Padilha, BBC.

Survivors of the Rainforest (1994). Director Andy Jillings, Zephyr Films.

The Sanema (2005). Director Jonathan Clay, BBC.

MUSIC

A. Reahu He. *Cantos da Festa Yanomami/Songs from Yanomami Ceremonies and Rituals.* This unique CD was co-produced by the Yanomami organization Hutukara to raise funds for its projects. It is available from Hutukara and Survival International.

Great Barrier Reef Marine Park, Australia
National Parks, Changes in Perception, and Hyper-Reality

Celmara Pocock, Ph.D.
University of Southern Queensland, Australia

The Great Barrier Reef Marine Park Authority manages the largest living thing on Earth: the Great Barrier Reef off the coast of Queensland, Australia. Agricultural runoff, predatory starfish, local and global effects of climate change, increased sea temperatures, and ocean acidity threaten this spectacular coral reef. But increasingly, another more insidious degradation is also taking place. Direct sensuous experiences of the Reef are being displaced by substitutes that seem more authentic than the Reef itself. In the past, visitors to the islands and reefs enjoyed embodied encounters: touch, sound, sight, smell, and taste combined in an oriented experience that created a strong sense of place. Now human encounters are shaped by media and technology, distancing visitors from unique Reef environments. Despite unprecedented access to the underwater, tourists today are more likely to experience the Reef through secondary visual representations, such as photographs and films. These enhanced and brilliant images create a hyper-reality in which the copies appear more wondrous than the real thing.

Great Barrier Reef Marine Park: Changes in Perception

I wandered over it amazed at the colours of the corals, the shellfish and the tiny darting fish and crimson and blue slugs and stars and clams in its pool-gardens, and stared down from a small boat at its shelfs and coral crags. I fell in love with the Reef then, through that small and southmost part of it.

—Judith Wright, Australian poet and Great Barrier Reef activist, *The Coral Battleground*, 1977

Great Barrier Reef Marine Park and World Heritage Area

The Great Barrier Reef is treasured as a World Heritage site for its exceptional visual beauty, including brilliantly colored marine life and magnificent aerial vistas. The Great Barrier Reef Marine Park Authority was established in 1975 to manage this largest living entity on Earth. The region comprises a chain of coral reefs, islands, and cays that stretch 2,300 kilometers along the northeast coast of Australia—almost the distance between Moscow and London.

The Reef is a sensitive indicator of climate change, and a barometer of our planet's health. Corals are delicate living organisms, closely related to jellyfish and anemones. Hard corals comprise colonies of miniscule polyps that form protective, calcified skeletons. These tiny animals gradually build

Left: **Corals and bright yellow sponge** on the Reef slope at an unidentified location.
K. Swalling © Commonwealth of Australia (GBRMPA)

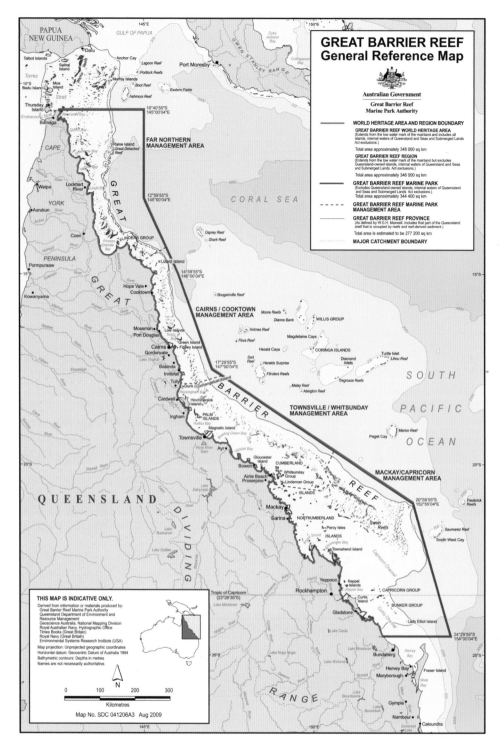

**GREAT BARRIER REEF
General Reference Map**

Australian Government

Great Barrier Reef
Marine Park Authority

	WORLD HERITAGE AREA AND REGION BOUNDARY
	GREAT BARRIER REEF WORLD HERITAGE AREA (Extends from the low water mark of the mainland and includes all islands, internal waters of Queensland and Seas and Submerged Lands Act exclusions.)
	Total area approximately 348 000 sq km
	GREAT BARRIER REEF REGION (Extends from the low water mark of the mainland but excludes Queensland-owned islands, internal waters of Queensland and Seas and Submerged Lands Act exclusions.)
	Total area approximately 346 000 sq km
	GREAT BARRIER REEF MARINE PARK (Excludes Queensland-owned islands, internal waters of Queensland and Seas and Submerged Lands Act exclusions.)
	Total area approximately 344 400 sq km
- - - -	**GREAT BARRIER REEF MARINE PARK MANAGEMENT AREA**
	GREAT BARRIER REEF PROVINCE (As defined by W.G.H. Maxwell. Includes that part of the Queensland shelf that is occupied by reefs and reef-derived sediment.)
	Total area is estimated to be 277 200 sq km
	MAJOR CATCHMENT BOUNDARY

THIS MAP IS INDICATIVE ONLY.
Derived from information or materials produced by:
Great Barrier Reef Marine Park Authority
Queensland Department of Environment and
Resource Management
Geoscience Australia, National Mapping Division
Royal Australian Navy, Hydrographic Office
Times Books (Great Britain)
Royal Navy (Great Britain)
Environmental Systems Research Institute (USA)

Map projection: Unprojected geographic coordinates
Horizontal datum: Geocentric Datum of Australia 1994
Bathymetric contours: Depths in metres
Names are not necessarily authoritative.

0   100   200   300
Kilometres

Map No. SDC 041206A3 Aug 2009

Previous pages: **The magical quality of the underwater reef** with its brilliant colors and variety of life captivates the mind, heart, and imagination. Immersed in a cloud of yellowtailed demoiselle fishes (*Neopomacentrus azysron*), a diver explores the colorful plate and branched corals (*Acropora sp.*) and feather stars (*Oxycomanthus bennetti*) at Bowl Reef, central section of the Great Barrier Reef.
D. McKillop ©Commonwealth of Australia (GBRMPA)

Left: **Map of the Great Barrier Reef** showing the boundaries of the Marine Park and World Heritage Area. These extend from the low water mark of the Queensland coast to the edge of the continental shelf and encompass all islands.
© *Commonwealth of Australia (GBRMPA)*

intricate rock-like structures, the unique ecosystems of the Great Barrier Reef that provide shelter for brilliant marine life.

Corals are sensitive to mechanical damage and changes in the environment. The Great Barrier Reef Marine Park Authority employs a zoning system to manage the multiple uses of the region, working with industry and user groups to regulate and restrict activities and minimize local impacts. It has successfully reduced immediate threats such as anchor damage and overfishing to ensure the health of the Reef today. The future challenge is to adapt management strategies to ameliorate the larger and more uncertain effects of climate change.

View of ENDEAVOUR RIVER, *on the* Coast *of* New-Holland, *where* Captain Cook *had the* Ship *laid on Shore, in order to repair the Damage which she received on the Rock.*

Above: **Scene of the *Endeavour*** laid on shore for repairs following a collision with the Great Barrier Reef, 1770.

G. W. Anderson 1786 © National Library of Australia

RIght: Early in the 20th century **scientists investigated the natural history** of the islands, coast, and corals of the Reef by living on the islands for several weeks at a time. Sixteen-year-old Dene Fry accompanied scientists from the Australian Museum to the Capricorn Islands in 1910. Their laboratory was set up outside, surrounded by the native vegetation.

© Mitchell Library, State Library of New South Wales

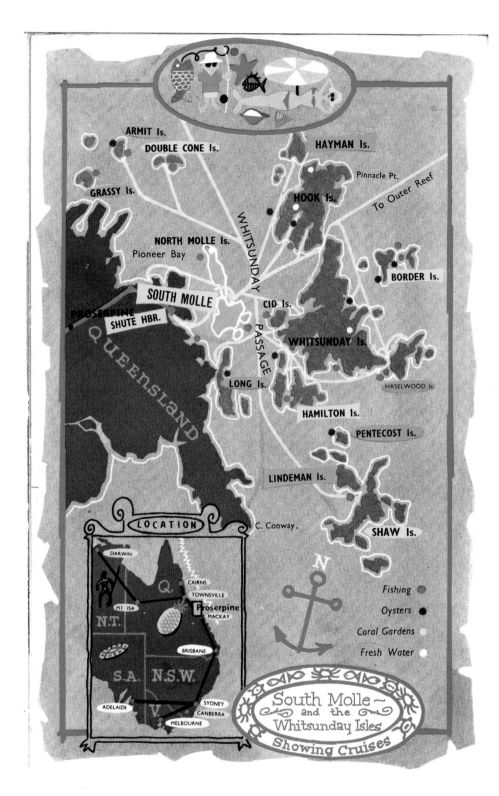

Left: **Tourist maps** like this one from the Whitsundays Islands in the 1950s helped visitors understand their location at the Reef and its relationship to other islands and attractions.
© *Private Collection*

Above right: **Tourism at the Reef was reinvigorated in the 1950s** and expanded rapidly in the 1960s and 1970s. Corals and shells were popular holiday souvenirs, but fossicking or reefing had detrimental effects. The activity was widespread and even promoted, as seen in this postcard from the 1960s. The current prohibition of unlicensed collecting is vital to the health of the Reef, but has reduced tactile encounters with, and knowledge of, marine life.
© *Centre for the Government of Queensland, about 1960*

Right: **The coconut, a potent symbol of an imagined paradise,** was used to signify the Reef as a tropical location and was propagated within tourist areas. Surrounded by native vegetation, this tourist poses with a coconut at Scawfell Island in 1933, fulfilling her desire for a tropical island of romantic fiction.
R.M. Berryman © National Library of Australia

Climate change threatens the well-being of the Reef in several ways. More frequent and intense cyclones and floods exacerbate existing water quality problems as more sediments, pesticides, and nutrients flow to Reef waters from agricultural land on the adjacent Australian coast. These create biological imbalances and outbreaks, including suffocating algae and a population explosion of destructive crown-of-thorn starfish. Higher atmospheric carbon levels lead to increased ocean acidity, and global warming increases sea levels and ocean temperatures. Together they wreak untold damage on coral growth, irrevocably alter the distribution and diversity of coral species, and dramatically

Collecting Coral and Shells, on the reef

Like physical threats, changes in human perceptions threaten to irrevocably alter the Reef, transforming it from a meaningful and valued place into a non-place.

Navigation: Fear and Danger

All the dangers we had escaped were little in comparison of being thrown upon this reef, where the Ship must be dashed to pieces in a Moment. A reef such as one speaks of here is Scarcely known in Europe. It is a Wall of Coral Rock rising almost perpendicular out of the unfathomable Ocean, always overflown at high Water generally 7 or 8 feet, and dry in places at Low Water. The Large Waves of the Vast Ocean meeting with so sudden a resistance makes a most Terrible Surf, breaking Mountains high, especially as in our case, when the General Trade Wind blows directly upon it.

> —Captain James Cook,
> Aug. 16, 1770

For the earliest European navigators, the east coast of Australia was an unknown and frightening experience. The endless and unexplored shoals, cays, and reefs posed significant dangers to early ships. The voyage of Captain James Cook narrowly escaped disaster when the *Endeavour* collided with a submerged reef in 1770. The party was forced to stop for six weeks while repairs were made at the eponymous Endeavour River. Saving the ship and successfully navigating a safe passage through the labyrinth of uncharted shoals and reefs affirmed Cook's reputation as a master navigator.

Today tourists pay scant attention to the routes or orientation that bring them to their Reef destination.

change interactions within closely woven ecosystems.

Another less obvious threat to the Reef is that of changes in human perception. Diminished senses of orientation and first-hand encounters have gradually changed how the region is understood and valued.

Curiosity: Touch and Thrill

I can hardly imagine one being happier than when taking a stroll at low spring tide on the Barrier Reef, with its wealth of shells, corals, crabs, sea-urchins, beche-de-mer, *and other strange things that only a naturalist could classify. Every stone one turns over reveals material for a collection; every piece of live coral broken off seems to add its share; not only the polyp which made the structure, but the weird and wonderful tiny crabs, shrimps, and little fish that make their homes among the branching coral. Everything seems to be teeming with life. And it is not necessary to be a naturalist to enjoy these wonders; anyone with a love of nature would be thrilled.*

—A. F. Ellis, *Adventuring in Coral Seas*, 1936

The first scientific observations of the Reef were made during 19th- and 20th-century voyages of discovery, and science rapidly became integral to perceptions of the region. The earliest holidaymakers participated in scientific collecting and recording, and tourists fossicked for their own shell and coral collections. They amassed thousands of specimens and acquired an intimate knowledge of coral and shell habitats, the feel of living animals, and sensuous knowledge of islands and reefs.

Tropical Islands: Romance and Literature

Most people have a mental picture of a coral island in a tropical setting of palm trees, of the crystal-clear water of a lagoon where multi-hued fish and other forms of colourful marine life abound, and where life may be idled away with the cares of the world forgotten. Every effort should therefore be made to present this picture to the tourist in actual reality, otherwise he may leave the Reef disappointed by his experience, with consequences that will be anything but fruitful.

—Theodore C. Roughley, 1947

Above: **As tourism grew on the islands**, purpose-built accommodation strived to meet an imagined and idealized tropical destination, as suggested by the style and building materials used in these grass huts on Lindeman Island in the 1930s.
Australian National Travel Association © National Archives of Australia

Above: **The exclusive Hayman Island Resort** presents tourists with an idealized tropical island holiday destination. Air-conditioned luxury, manicured exotic gardens, and swimming pools overlooking the coral seas distance visitors from the natural environment.
© *Hayman Island Resort*

Despite the Australian bush setting of the early camps, visitors imagined a tropical landscape based on images from romantic fiction and artistic impressions of the South Sea Islands. These idealized landscapes gradually became a reality as tourist resorts developed to fulfill the desires for an imaginary idyll.

Camping is still available on some islands in the marine park, but this is barely promoted. Most visitors make daytrips from tourist centers on the adjacent mainland, or stay in one of the many resorts on the islands. The most popular and accessible resorts have swimming pools, air-conditioned accommodations, and landscaped grounds that mimic idealized tropical islands. Visitors who stay within these artificial environments may never experience the sights, sounds, and smells of the unique native vegetation.

Underwater: Representation and Invention

Quaintly-formed and gaily-coloured coral fishes were seen in the deep pools in water of astounding transparency. We saw the beautiful shells of which we had read, including the clams with the flesh of their expanded bodies displaying every conceivable combination of colours. All these, and the indescribable beauty of the live coral, satisfied us that we had not listened in vain to our urge.
> —H. D. Fletcher, "The Island of Desire," *Bank Notes*, 1935

Part of the allure of the underwater coral gardens is their inaccessibility to humans. A constant evolution of technology has provided increased access to this unfamiliar space. Visitors today have unprecedented access to the underwater. Once the preserve of scientists and professional photographers, diving became more accessible in the 1960s and 1970s. Snorkelling provides a fully immersed experience with relatively

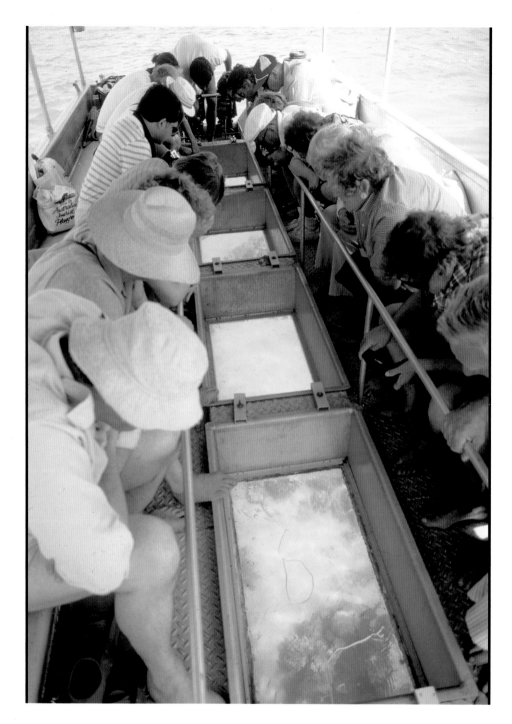

Previous pages: **Diving provides the most intimate of encounters** with the underwater. Weightless and freed of the constraints of land, divers with air-tanks become integrated into this extraordinary world. The technology and skill required and its resonance with marine science make diving a personal bodily experience.
K. Hoppen © Commonwealth of Australia (GBRMPA)

Left: **Glass-bottomed boats** allow visitors to view the Reef over deeper water and share the view with one another. Recent innovations allow night voyages that give visitors extraordinary glimpses of extended polyps and nocturnal movements.
© Commonwealth of Australia (GBRMPA)

simple, low-maintenance equipment and basic skills. The shallow waters of many coral reefs of the Great Barrier Reef make it accessible and popular with tourists. Take only photographs....

Divers grope with words to express the gap between the experience and the recollection. The diver wants to latch onto and hold the feeling of being there. This helps explain the popularity of underwater photography. To me, holding

camera gear gets in the way of actually "being there," but to many, film conveys better than words the immediacy of the underwater experience.
—Rosaleen Love, *Reefscape: Reflections on the Great Barrier Reef,* 2001

Hyper-Reality and Authentic Fakes
People are sold on seeing this wonderful footage of brilliant coral and thousands of coral reef fish, then they go and swim

Right: **Snorkelers drift across the clear blue waters** of Nathan Reef. Snorkelers can view the corals and fishes from above or make quick dives to short depths to share the perspective of the inhabitants.
A. Rankin © Commonwealth of Australia (GBRMPA)

on a reef that has been eaten out for example by crown-of-thorns [starfish].
—Col McKenzie, Executive Director, Association of Marine Park Tourism Operators, September 2009

Your next trip to the Great Barrier Reef could be from the comfort of your home.
—engadget.com, 2012

Heron Island's number one attraction is the marine life, diving and snorkelling. I went snorkelling every day. I saw amazing

varieties of fish and huge quantities and colours—just like what you would see on a David Attenborough documentary.
—Joshua Weir, 2009

The snorkelling (and diving) I did at the Outer Great Barrier Reef ... was like a National Geographic movie.
—girlstravelblog.com, 2010

Early visitor experiences of the Great Barrier Reef were characterized by long journeys, camping among native

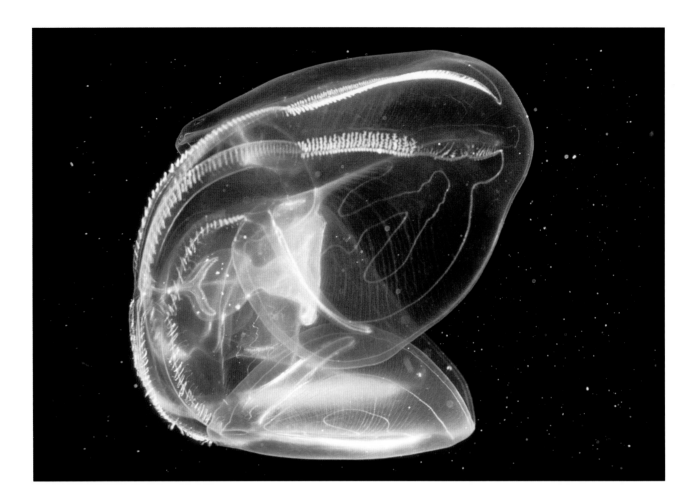

vegetation, and learning about the corals and reefs through collecting. In this way people came to know particular localities; the unique sounds, smells, and sights; tactile encounters and taste sensations that made each unique. They socialized together and shared their experiences to create a meaningful sense of place. In contrast, tourism by the end of the 20th century had become dislocated and dissociated from the environments of the islands, the reefs, and the human interactions that made Reef locations meaningful places.

Today elaborate pontoons replete with kiosks and souvenir shops are moored on the Outer Reef, traditionally the most exciting, dangerous, and difficult area to access. Tourists now visit these extremes in all but the worst weather conditions, no longer reliant on tides, seasons, or winds. The exciting navigational adventures to the Outer Reef are now made tolerable by diversions such as videos, bars, and

snacks. On these safe artificial islands, few seem aware of how remote and deep the surrounding waters actually are. Tourists often get a distorted view of the actual condition of the Reef because they only visit controlled and selected areas.

Aquariums are a popular way to portray the Reef and they are a convenient space in which to capture images of more elusive species. Aquariums are artificial environments that are compared to the natural world, while the Reef itself is increasingly compared to these contrived and technologically sustained tanks, as in a 2010 promotion proclaiming the "Great Barrier Reef—Discover the world's largest natural aquarium."

Photography brings the underwater Reef to us more brilliantly and more intimately than most will ever experience in person. Taken at extraordinary depths, or in areas inaccessible to tourists, many images are captured at night when corals are

Previous pages: **Sophisticated underwater cameras**, lighting, color emulsion, and digital imagery produce extraordinary images of the underwater corals. They startle us with the magnificence of the colors, shapes, and diversity of marine life.
B. Cropp © Commonwealth of Australia (GBRMPA)

Above: **The extraordinary detail of microscopic reef life**, like this comb jelly (*Ctenophora*), is made visible through state-of-the-art technologies unmatched by the human eye.
M. Jones © Commonwealth of Australia (GBRMPA)

Next pages: **Aerial photography** simultaneously encapsulates multiple forms into a single frame, offering magnificent cartographic views in which the Reef is represented as a single entity.
W. Stewart © Commonwealth of Australia (GBRMPA)

fully extended and at their most brilliant. Access to these conditions is as technical and contrived as the early images created by William Saville-Kent. They do not represent the experience of being on the Reef. For some, visiting the Reef itself can appear disappointing.

Technologies are becoming as important as firsthand experiences of the Reef. Reef images can be shared almost instantaneously with people anywhere so that interactions in cyberspace overshadow the immediate, emplaced relationships between people and between people and Reef environments. The hyper-real Reef can be created and enjoyed anywhere. It does not rely on continuance of the Great Barrier Reef or conservation of the marine park. The Reef may be left vulnerable as it loses its connection with those who love it from direct encounters.

Where to Learn More

BOOKS

Rosaleen Love. *Reefscape: Reflections on the Great Barrier Reef*. St. Leonards, Australia: Allen & Unwin, 2000.

J. Bowen and M. Bowen. *The Great Barrier Reef: history, science, heritage*. Cambridge: Cambridge University Press, 2002.

Celmara Pocock. "Blue Lagoons and Coconut Palms": The Creation of a Tropical Idyll in Australia. *The Australian Journal of Anthropology,* vol. 16, no. 3 (2005), pp. 335-49.

Pocock, Celmara. "Entwined Histories: Photography and Tourism at the Great Barrier Reef" in M. Robinson and D. Picard, eds., *The framed world: tourism, tourists and photography*. Farnham, England and Burlington, Vt.: Ashgate Publishing, 2009, pp. 185-97.

WHAT'S HAPPENING WITH CORAL REEFS

International Coral Reef Initiative (ICRI), a partnership of government, international, and non-government organizations aiming to preserve coral reefs and related ecosystems.
http://www.icriforum.org/

Australian Institute of Marine Science (AIMS) is a leader in tropical marine science.
www.aims.gov.au

GET INVOLVED

The Great Barrier Reef Marine Park Authority website provides information on how you can get involved and what you can do to protect the Reef. It includes educational resources for schools and an extensive photographic library.
www.gbrmpa.gov.au

IF YOU GO

There are many options for visitors to the Great Barrier Reef. The two major mainland centers for tourism activities are Cairns in the far north and Airlie Beach in the Whitsundays Islands region. Smaller tours can offer a more low-key experience and a closer encounter with the islands and reefs. Choose a resort or tour that is accredited through the Great Barrier Reef Marine Park Authority or accredited through the Australian Ecotourism Association.
www.ecotourism.org.au

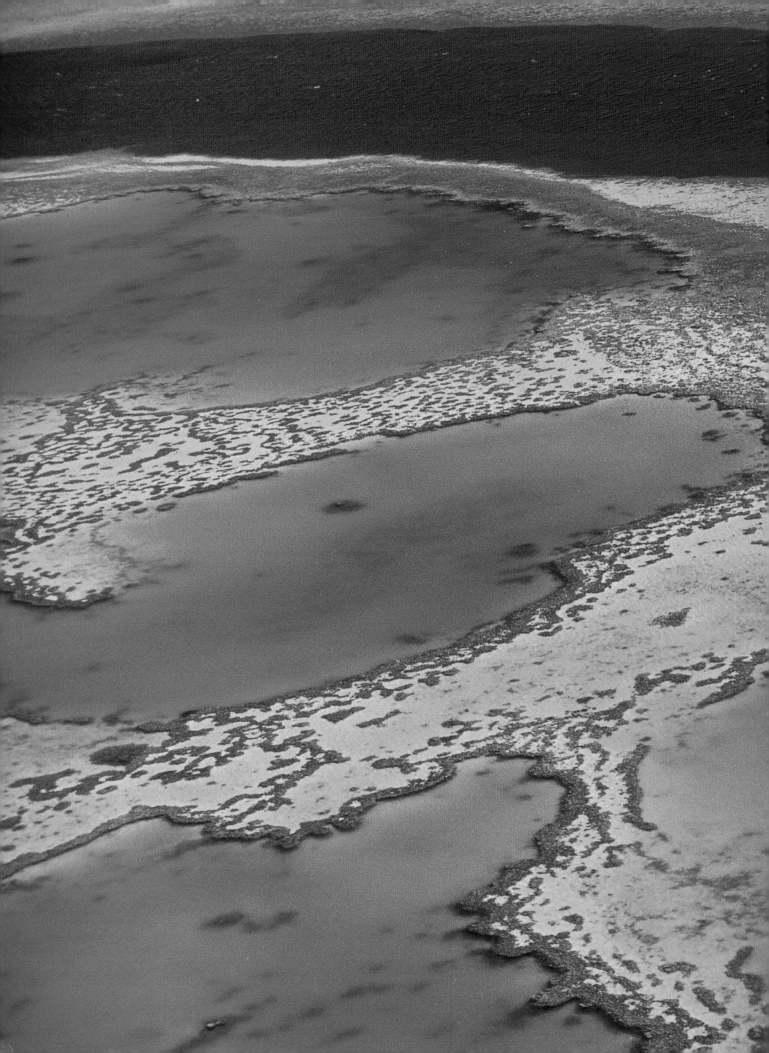

Changes in the Scientific Understanding of Nature

Can National Parks Be Preserved "Unimpaired"?

Randolph Delehanty, Ph.D.

Historian, Presidio Trust, Golden Gate National Recreation Area, San Francisco

Human activity is changing the world in profound ways. Few ecologists now think that "natural" processes will automatically lead to "natural" results in a world characterized by pollution, global warming, habitat fragmentation, invasive plants and animals, the loss of top predators, and the extinction of species. The current ecological paradigm does not assume that nature is stable or that it automatically produces equilibrium. Leading-edge thinkers are disabusing us of the romantic notion of "wildness." National parks and protected-area managers are struggling to keep up with advances in environmental science. The National Park Service has recently revised its definition of "unimpaired." Pioneer plant ecologist Frank Egler (1911–1996) contended that "ecosystems are not only more complex than we think, they are more complex than we *can* think."[1]

Research ecologist Nate Stephenson of the Biological Resources Division of the U.S. Geological Survey proposes a new approach to protected areas, recognizing that degradation is inevitable and that preserving resources "unimpaired" is not possible. He does not assume that the ecological world is stable or that it produces equilibrium. Park managers, he proposes, should redirect their thinking in order to preserve as much native biodiversity as possible while realizing that some species will be lost. Practices that are currently rejected— assisting the migration of native species to new locations in the face of global warming, planting species that fail to reproduce on their own, and irrigating "wild" areas—may need to be adopted. Such interventionist management flatly contradicts the assumptions of 19th- and 20th-century park advocates who thought that natural resources could be preserved "unimpaired," as if under a glass dome. This interventionist approach has its roots in the A. Starker Leopold Report commissioned by Department of the Interior Secretary Stewart Udall in 1963. Stephenson's critics warn that, so far, attempts to manipulate ecosystems have often had negative unintended consequences.

This new view has erased any notion of going back to a presumed pristine condition. Decisions about where and how to intervene in ecosystems face an unpredictable future, including the unintended impacts of conscious

Left: In spite of a severe climate, **summer in the Chang Tang offers bright flowers** such as this lousewort (Pedicularis).
Photo by George B. Schaller

interventions. The stewards of protected areas are working in a world of increasing uncertainty. Nature, ecologists stress, is in constant flux. The only possible response is to be flexible and to pursue what's called "adaptive management." Careful monitoring of park manager interventions with the goal of learning from them is the new future for parks. These experimental interventions must be executed in a context of radical uncertainty. It is, indeed, a brave new world lacking the simple comforts of the past, which presumed that nature always seeks a balance. The conservation of biodiversity, while easily proclaimed, is extremely difficult to achieve in reality, given the dynamism of ecosystems. The U.S. Endangered Species Act of 1973 requires that *all* threatened and endangered species be recovered. This is not possible. *Which* species are to be conserved is the question. *How* can they be conserved? What are the priorities if all cannot be conserved? Who sets priorities when goals conflict? What are the various roles of scientists, politicians, and interested members of the public in setting these goals?

Networks and Corridors

Fires, floods, and wildlife (and now plant) migrations do not stop at park boundaries. Current thinking in protected areas is to look out rather than just in, to consider the context in which a park is set, not just the park itself. Complete ecosystems, and even larger regional or continental landscapes, need to be considered. R. F. Noss, provost's distinguished research professor at the University of Central Florida, has proposed that park managers consider ecological networks of conservation areas and surrounding buffer zones

connected by corridors. These corridors allow migration and genetic exchange and allow ecological processes to function over very large areas.

Today there are over 500 UNESCO biosphere reserves in more than 100 countries. The United States Congress, however, has refused to join UNESCO's "Man and the Biosphere" program, fearing a loss of sovereignty. The Convention on Biological Diversity of 2004 called for an international system of protected areas. Buffer areas would allow some resource extraction and the economic activities of human populations, such as farming and herding. This is akin to the situation of national parks surrounded by larger national forests in the western United States. The Wildlands Project, an NGO organized in 1991, proposes that 50 percent of North America be declared "wild land" to preserve biological diversity. It proposes four "megalinks" across North America: the Pacific Megalink (Baja, California to Alaska), the Spine of the Continent Megalinkage (Mesoamerica to Alaska), the Atlantic Megalinkage (Florida to New Brunswick) and the Boreal Megalinkage (Maritime Provinces of Canada to Alaska). There is also a proposed Pan-European Ecological Network across 52 nation-states in Europe and northern Asia, and the Gondwana Link in southwestern Australia. Right now, these are just grandiose proposals, but they show the thinking of big-picture park proponents.[2]

The old question of too-small park boundaries is resurfacing now as plants, as well as animals, migrate in response to climate and precipitation changes. Are migrating species to be considered "invasive"? Managers of protected areas must find ways to work across jurisdictional boundaries. As anyone who has worked in government agencies knows, this is easier said than done. Different government agencies often have different bureaucratic cultures. It is sometimes the case that protecting the jurisdiction and preserving the traditional ways of the agency (not to mention budgets and jobs) take precedence over solving problems. Only the Wildlife Refuge System Improvement Act of 1997 requires cooperation across agencies. How successful has this been? How are conflicts among government agencies to be resolved? Conservation questions, like other legal issues, often get caught up in extraneous political and personality issues in the messy sausage factory of law-making. Goals need to be set collaboratively among many agencies. But too often this only results in bland agreements that respond to the politics of organizations without improving the level of resource protection. (This is also the case with too many international environmental accords.) The division between public lands and private lands remains a fundamental challenge in preserving critical habitat in ambitious regional conservation plans. Public protected lands are, of course, set within the much larger context of private properties. In the U.S., 60 percent of all land is privately owned.

Ecosystems and Global Interconnections

Environmental and ecological knowledge continue to make advances in discovering and explaining the myriad of interconnections in the natural world. A consequence of this is that managers of protected areas now look beyond their parks' borders to consider the larger ecosystems within which they are set.

The Greater Yellowstone Ecosystem is a good example. It embraces two national parks, six national forests, and three national wildlife refuges totaling 14 million acres. An additional 5 million acres of private land round out the Greater Yellowstone Ecosystem. Real coordination has yet to happen in the ecosystem. The Park Service continues its biodiversity preservationist practices on its lands, while the Forest Service continues its "wise use" policies and leases out oil and gas reserves on its lands.

On a global scale, what ecological scientists study is the vast web of life in the entire natural world. Compelled by this global vision, environmentalists press for stronger measures in everything from air pollution control to forbidding the importation of "exotic" species, and not just in protected areas. Despite the existence of the United Nations and organizations such as the International Union of Conservation of Nature (IUCN), and the lofty goals of various international environmental accords— the 1992 Convention on Biological Diversity adopted in Rio de Janeiro or the 1997 Kyoto Protocol that sought to reduce releases of greenhouse gasses below 1990 levels—the entities directly responsible for environmental protection continue to be individual nation-states. (The Copenhagen environmental summit of 2009 failed to reach any meaningful agreement at all.) Nation-states vary greatly in their levels of economic development from rich to destitute, and in their ability to enforce agreements and to police their territories that range from highly competent to the anarchy rampant in failed states. But nation-states also vary greatly in the influence of environmentalist values on their domestic politics. A few wealthy countries with well-educated populations, such as Canada, the Netherlands, and Denmark, are quite advanced in their acceptance of environmental protection and in the strength of the domestic political consensus behind these measures. At the other end of the spectrum, in places like Burundi, farmers are invading national parks and treating them as agricultural frontiers, thus destroying them. Other nations, including the United States and China, refuse to back mandatory reductions in pollutants and propose only voluntary measures to reduce emissions.

Today global recession is seen as yet one more obstacle to stronger environmental action. Thus, while environmental science calls for more stringent controls over larger areas—indeed the entire globe— powerful economic interests arguing for economic growth block legislative measures that they fear will add to the cost of doing business or that make raw materials more expensive. The deeply disturbing question arises: Can democratic governments with their short-time horizons deal effectively with the long-term threats we face?

In the U.S., the National Park Service traditionally has been underfunded even in times when the mainstream political consensus supported national parks. Today the costs of employee benefits, of the increasing number of higher-paid managers, and general price inflation are exacerbating park budget problems. Normal wear and tear resulted in a maintenance backlog of $1.9 billion in 1988; it grew to $4 to $6 billion by 2002. The NPS budget has been reduced by 6 percent since 2010, including a cut of $139 million in FY2011.[3] The Park Service has coped over the last decade by shifting money

from maintenance and land acquisition to day-to-day operations. In 2001, operations constituted 64 percent of total park appropriations; in 2013 they consumed 87 percent of congressional appropriations. This has left the national parks with an $11.4 billion backlog of needed construction and maintenance projects across the system.

Parks Canada and the Goal of Ecological Integrity

Despite difficulties, progress continues in the world of environmental science. The new goal among contemporary park managers is *ecological integrity*. Integrity means that ecological systems are whole and functioning well. Ecosystems are not static; they change over both the short and long term. Ecosystem stewards seek to maintain native biodiversity, intact food chains, and the processes that support native species. Different scientists define ecological integrity in different ways. Canada's National Park Act of 1998 defines ecological integrity as "a condition that is determined to be characteristic of its natural region and likely to persist, including abiotic [nonliving] components [such as light, temperature, and atmospheric gases] and the composition and abundance of native species and biological communities, rates of change and supporting processes." Ecological integrity has replaced the vague idea of "naturalness" as the goal of national park management in Canada. Among the characteristics of protected areas with ecological integrity are that they have a full complement of native species; that their food webs are long and complex; that they maintain their structural integrity by degrading energy while avoiding entropy; and that they retain their nutrient pools. Ecological integrity replaces more generalized nature protection goals with specific and measurable endpoints. Monitoring on a regular and continuous basis allows park managers to gauge the success or failure of their efforts. In Canada, each park uses monitored data to produce a "State of the Park" report every five years. These are public accountability documents that make explicit the direction(s) of park management. The ecological integrity approach presumes active management and planned restoration programs. It gives a systematic context to the goal of preserving biodiversity. Ecological integrity accepts that humans, including aboriginal peoples, have been integral to most of the ecosystems in protected areas. It also recognizes the dynamism of nature and of man's role within it.

The challenges that national parks and other protected areas face in a rapidly changing world are many and can seem daunting, if not overwhelming. Parks are the canaries in the coal mine of the modern world. We must always keep in mind that they are political creations and require dedicated political engagement to survive and even flourish. How our and subsequent generations respond to these challenges will be a measure of our sense of responsibility to ourselves and to the future. Those who understand the ecological and social value of great parks must speak up for them. Humanity's calling is no longer the ancient one of "subduing" the Earth; it is to understand it and protect its diversity of life.

Notes

1. Eric S. Higgs and Richard J. Hobbs, "Wild Design: Principles to Guide Interventions in Protected Areas" in David N. Cole and Laurie Yung, eds., *Beyond Naturalness: Rethinking Park and Wilderness Stewardship in an Era of Rapid Change.* Washington: Island Press, 2012, p. 242 [emphasis added].

2. Ibid., p. 205.

3. *New York Times,* Aug. 28, 2011, p. 14.

Appendix

Definitions of Protected Areas

In 1971, the International Union of Conservation of Nature, headquartered in Gland, Switzerland, defined a national park as a place:

● with one or more ecosystems not materially altered by human exploitation and occupation where plant and animal species, geomorphological sites, and habitats are of special scientific, educative, and recreational interest or which contain a natural landscape of great beauty

● where the highest competent authority of the country has taken steps to prevent or eliminate as soon as possible exploitation or occupation in the whole area and to enforce effectively the respect for the ecological, geomorphological, or aesthetic features which have led to its establishment

● where visitors are allowed to enter, under special conditions, for inspirational, educational, cultural, and recreational purposes

● that has a minimum size of 1,000 hectares (2,471 acres) within zones in which protection of nature takes precedence

● has statutory protection

● has a budget and staff sufficient to provide effective protection

● prohibits exploitation of natural resources (including the development of dams) qualified by such activities as sports, fishing, the need for management, facilities, etc.

The IUCN classifies the wide variety of protected areas under five categories.

CATEGORY IA

Strict Nature Reserve: protected area of land or sea managed mainly for scientific research and/or environmental monitoring.

CATEGORY IB

Wilderness Area: large protected area of land or sea managed mainly for wilderness protection and without permanent or significant habitation.

CATEGORY II

National Park: protected natural area of land or sea managed mainly for ecosystem protection and recreation. The area is designated to (a) protect the ecological integrity of one or more ecosystems for present and future generations, (b) exclude exploitation or occupation inimical to the purposes of designation of the area, and (c) provide a foundation for spiritual, scientific, educational, recreational, and visitor opportunities, all of which must be environmentally and culturally compatible.

CATEGORY III

Natural Monument: protected area managed mainly for the conservation of a specific natural or natural/cultural feature which is of outstanding or unique value because of its inherent rarity, representative or aesthetic qualities, or cultural significance.

CATEGORY IV

Habitat/Species Management Area: a protected area managed mainly for conservation through management intervention. An area of land or sea subject to active intervention for management purposes so as to ensure the maintenance of habitats and/or to meet the requirements of specific species.

CATEGORY V

Protected Landscape/Seascape: a protected area managed mainly for landscape/seascape conservation and recreation. An area of land, with coast and sea as appropriate, where the interaction of people and nature over time has produced an area of distinct character with significant aesthetic, ecological, and/or cultural value, and often with high biological diversity. Safeguarding the integrity of this traditional interaction is vital to the protection, maintenance, and evolution of such an area.

CATEGORY VI

Managed Resource Protected Area: a protected area managed mainly for the sustainable use of natural ecosystems. An area containing predominantly unmodified natural systems, managed to ensure long-term protection and maintenance of biological diversity, while providing at the same time a sustainable flow of natural products and services to meet community needs.

Contributors

Randolph Delehanty, Ph.D., is the historian at the Presidio Trust, a federal agency responsible for the interior 80 percent of the Presidio of San Francisco within the Golden Gate National Recreation Area. He holds degrees in history from Georgetown University, the University of Chicago, and Harvard University, where he earned his doctorate. He is the author of many books, including *Preserving the West* (National Trust for Historic Preservation), *San Francisco: The Ultimate Guide*, and *New Orleans: Elegance and Decadence*. He has also curated many exhibitions including "Plants + Insects / Art + Science," "War & Dissent: The U.S. in the Philippines, 1898–1915," and "Crown Jewels: Five Great National Parks Around the World and the Challenges They Face."

"Parks are among the greatest of human political creations and embody important social, scientific, and spiritual values. I can envision all of the oceans, atmosphere, and outer space as future protected areas. I myself feel most alive in historic cities that respect their past and in parks both large and small. Parks affirm that humankind can act responsibly toward the Earth. They give me wonder and hope."

George B. Schaller, Ph.D., is a noted field biologist and senior conservationist for the Wildlife Conservation Society, vice president of Panthera, an organization devoted to the conservation of the world's wild cats, and an adjunct professor with the Center of Nature and Society at Peking University in China. Born in Berlin, Germany, in 1933, he moved to Missouri as a teenager. He is a graduate of the University of Alaska and the University of Wisconsin, and has spent more than half a century studying wildlife and helping protect some of the planet's most endangered and iconic animals, from the mountain gorillas in the Congo to tigers in India, lions in Tanzania, jaguars in Brazil, giant pandas in China, and snow leopards, wild sheep, and goats in the Himalayas. He is the author of 16 books, including *Tibet Wild: A Naturalist's Journeys on the Roof of the World*. Dr. Schaller has conducted conservation projects in some 23 countries including Laos, Myanmar, Mongolia, Iran, and Tajikistan. He has helped establish about a dozen protected areas in various countries, including the Arctic National Wildlife Refuge in Alaska.

"I have specialized in studying the behavior and ecology of large mammals and in promoting their protection through the establishment of reserves, though I realized with time that most reserves are too small to survive under human pressure and now climate change. I now strive to protect whole landscapes. I went to the Chang Tang Reserve to study its wildlife. But I soon became enthralled with its landscape, wildlife, and people. Where else can one stand on a hill, the eyes sweeping across plains and distant snow ranges, and know that the land remains essentially intact? To bequeath an unimpaired Chang Tang to the future requires an understanding of its ecology and our never-ending vigilance. To assure continuity, I work with young Tibetan and Han Chinese who also devote themselves to the Tibetan Plateau and work to make certain that the chiru, the kiang, and all the others will continue to roam in security and freedom as part of China's—and the world's—natural heritage."

John R. F. Bower, Ph.D., has spent over 40 years researching prehistoric archeology. His experience ranges from work with materials from Olduvai Gorge to a comparative study of ice age archeology in Poland and the United States. His most concentrated research efforts have been in Kenya and Tanzania, particularly in the Serengeti National Park. He has also done underwater archeology in Israel and excavated a site in Cuba. Dr. Bower grew up in Bogota, Colombia. His early education was at Upper Canada College in Toronto, Canada. He holds an undergraduate degree in geology from Harvard College and a doctorate in anthropology from Northwestern University. He spent most of his teaching and research career at Iowa State University, where he is professor emeritus. Currently, he is a visiting professor at the University of California, Davis.

"Archeology is a global enterprise and embraces many avenues of scientific research. One of the major attractions of archeology for me is discovery—learning about previously unknown aspects of the past in various parts of the world. With the new cultural resource management laws that protect archeological sites in the United States, I believe that jobs for archeologists will continue to grow in the future."

Audax Mabulla, Ph.D., researches the evolution of Stone Age cultures in East Africa. He has done archeological work among the Hadza hunting and foraging cultural group at Lake Eyasi Basin for many years. He is working with an international team at Olduvai Gorge and Laetoli. He is well known for his interests in African rock art. Dr. Mabulla received his B.A. from the University of Dar es Salaam and his M.A. and Ph.D. in Anthropology from the University of Florida. He is an associate professor

in the Department of History and Archeology at the University of Dar es Salaam, where he has held various lecturing and administrative positions. Dr. Mabulla's collaboration with Dr. John Bower spans approximately 10 years as co-investigator of an open-air site in the Serengeti National Park known as Loiyangalani. They are the authors of "Cultural Heritage Management in Tanzania's Protected Areas: Challenges and Prospects" in *CRM: The Journal of Heritage Stewardship*, Winter 2010.

JUDITH HARRIS is a writer based in Rome and the author of *Pompeii Awakened: A Story of Rediscovery*. For 25 years she conducted weekly radio broadcasts on Italian culture—especially archeology—for the Italian national network RAI. She has written for the *Wall Street Journal, Time, ARTnews,* and *Archeological Odyssey.* Her "beat" includes archeology, art history, archeo/art theft and the Mafia. Educated in the U.S and Switzerland, she has lived in Italy for much of her life. She began her career as a U.S. cultural attaché in Rome.

"As a reporter, I am what is called an 'Italianist,' specialized in the daunting problems and myriad delights of Italy. After covering terrorism and the Mafia for decades, I decided to focus on the conservation and protection of the beauties of this splendidly creative country. Pompeii exemplifies both the marvels of Italian creativity and the daunting challenge of preserving a cultural heritage admired the world over."

FIONA WATSON is research and field director at Survival International in London. She has worked on many campaigns for indigenous peoples' rights, notably with the Yanomami, Guarani, and Awá of Brazil, and "Bushmen" of the Central Kalahari in Botswana. She worked with the Hutukara Yanomami Association and Davi Kopenawa Yanomami. Before joining Survival, she participated in a joint UK-Brazilian scientific project run by the Institute of Amazon Research (INPA) in Manaus and the Royal Geographical Society in London researching the social and environmental impacts of deforestation in the northern Amazonian state of Roraima in Brazil. She has an M.A. in Hispanic languages and literature from St. Andrews University, Scotland, and did fieldwork living in a Quechua community in the Peruvian Andes. She has lived in South Africa, Venezuela, and Brazil.

"As a child growing up in Africa, I was fascinated by the diversity of tribal peoples, especially their vibrant costumes, their singing and laughter, and the enormous range of sounds in their languages. That lit a flame. I have investigated many appalling human rights violations and atrocities against indigenous peoples but have also met many remarkable, brave, and visionary people. What has touched me most is tribal peoples' humanity, their humor and resilience. Surviving against the odds, they are for me an inspiring example of what it means to be human, and a vital and vibrant part of the rich tapestry of human diversity."

JOANNA EEDE is a writer and editorial consultant to Survival International. She has a particular interest in the relationship between man and nature, and tribal peoples. She has created and edited three environmental books and writes for international newspapers and magazines, often collaborating with photojournalists. She has a particular interest in the Hadza tribe of northern Tanzania, a country through which she has travelled extensively, and in the reindeer herding peoples of Mongolia and Siberia. In 2012 she joined a group of Innu on a trek on snowshoes through the interior of Quebec and Labrador. Eede has a B.A. in French from Exeter University, United Kingdom.

"I find it both reassuring and fascinating to know that in an increasingly homogenous world there are still peoples who live in harmony with their environments, who measure time by the cycles of the moon, who can gauge the type of Arctic ice by looking at patterns in the clouds, or who use the song of an African bird to guide them to bees' nests in baobab trees. Much of my interest in tribal peoples is about their deep sense of intimacy with nature. They do not need 'civilizing' or 'developing.' On the contrary, it is the widespread notion that they are 'backward' that needs re-evaluation."

CELMARA POCOCK, Ph.D., is lecturer in anthropology and Australian indigenous studies at the University of Southern Queensland in Toowoomba. She wrote her doctoral thesis, "Romancing the Reef: History, Heritage and the Hyper-Real," at James Cook University in Australia with support from the Cooperative Research Centre for the Great Barrier Reef. She has worked as a heritage and museum manager in state and commonwealth agencies and for Aboriginal community organizations in Tasmania, Western Australia, and Queensland. She has a long-standing interest in human relationships with the environment and has researched and published on matters related to environmental anthropology, cultural heritage, and tourism.

"People are an essential part of all environments and landscapes because it is people who give these places meaning. Meaning is created from patterned, shared, and embodied experiences of the world around us. Technology can dazzle us. It enables us to share and experience the world as never before, and it is a powerful tool for worldwide conservation campaigns. Most often, however, it is the local, experienced, and lifelong knowledge and understanding of these regions that make them matter. It is this knowledge that can best inform decisions, and when things matter, people fight to keep them."

Index

A

affiliated areas, 39

Africa, 3–4

African Americans, 47
    sites, 35

Air Quality Act, 28

Alaska, parks expansion, 32–34

Alaska National Interest Lands
    Conservation Act, 32

Albright, Horace, 25, 26

all-terrain vehicles (ATVs), 45–46

Alto-Orinoco Casiquiare Biosphere
    Reserve, 99, 102
    see also Yanomami

American Civic Association, 23

Antietam Battlefield, 18

Anza-Borrego Desert State Park, 12

Archeological and Historic
    Preservation Act, 29

archeological parks, Italy, 83–97

archeology
    conservation, 92, 94
    entertainment, 91
    Ngorongoro Conservation Area,
    71–73
    Serengeti, 80, 81

Arches National Park, 38, 41, 47

Arizona, 24

Army harbor defense reservations,
    32

associations, US, 20–21
    listed, 21–22

Australia, 5–6, 119–135

automobiles, 27

B

bear, Tibetan brown, 64, 64

bee-eater, long-billed, 71

Berlusconi, Silvio, 90

bighorn sheep, 38

biodiversity, 2, 139
    conservation, 34, 140

biosphere reserves, 99, 140

birds
    Great Blue heron rookery, 41
    long-billed bee-eater, 71
    native, 25
    Tibetan snowcock, 61

Birkenhead Park, 14

bison, American, 19

body casts, Pompeii, 89

Boscoreale, 92, 94

Bower, John R. F., 148

Brazil, 5, 99, 102–117
    citizenship, 114–115

Brown, Jerry, 13

Buddhism, 58, 59
    chorten, 58
    lama, 59
    monasteries, 68

buffer areas, 140

buildings, historic, 28, 29

Bureau of Indian Affairs, 10, 11

Bureau of Land Management, 9, 11

Bureau of Reclamation, 10, 11, 27

burns, controlled, 45

Bush, George W., 34–35, 46

Buttes de Chaumont, 14

C

California, 10, 12
    see also Yosemite National Park

California Department of Parks and
    Recreation, 13
    budget, 13

California Redwood Park, 12

California State Park Commission, 12

Cammerer, Arno B., 26

Camp Sheridan, 17

camping, Great Barrier Reef, 127

Canada, 142–143
    Niagara Falls, 14

Cape Hatteras National Seashore, 27

Carter, Jimmy, 32

cassiterite, 111

Catlin, George, 13, 15

CCPY (Pro Yanomami Commission),
    113, 115

Central Park, 14

Chang Tang
    challenges, 64–65
    spiritual values, 68
    villagers, 58

Chang Tang Nature Reserve, 5, 51–69
    administration, 68

Chapman, Frank, 25

Chattanooga National Military Park,
    18

Chickamauga National Military Park,
    18

China, 5
    Tibet, 51–69

Chinese medicine, traditional, 62, 65

chiru, 54, 55, 62, 62, 64, 65

chorten, 58

Church, Frederic Edwin, 14

Citizens' Advisory Commissions, 40

Civil Protection Agency, 90

Civil War battlefields, 18

Civil War Trust, 18

Civilian Conservation Corps, 27

Clarke, John R., 94

Clean Water Act, 29

climate change, 48
 China, 59
 Great Barrier Reef, 119, 124

Clinton, Bill, 34

collective title, Yanomami and
 Ye'Kuana, 114

Conness, John, 14

conservation easements. See land
 trusts, private

controlled burns, 45

converted land, by region, 4

Cook, Captain James, 125

cooperating associations, 40

coral, 122, 122, 124, 127, 130, 134

corridors, 140–141

Creative Act, 19

Crissy Army Airfield, 41

Cultural Heritage Ministry, 90, 91

D

Davi Kopenawa Yanomami, 110, 113,
 115

Delehanty, Randolph, 146

Department of Agriculture, 10
 Division of Forestry, 20

Department of Commerce, 10

Department of Defense, 10, 11

Department of the Interior, 9, 10, 21,
 33
 funding, 33

Department of Transportation Act,
 28

Devil's Tower National Monument, 20

Dinosaur National Monument, 27

diversity
 American people, 35
 park users, 47

diving, 130, 130

Dobbins, John, 94

dogs, Pompeii, 90

Drury, Newton B., 27

E

easements, 41, 44

ecological integrity, 142–143

ecology, 28–29, 139

ecosystems, 99, 141

education, NPS, 48

Eede, Joanna, 150

Ellis, A. F., 126

Ellis, Steven, 94

Endangered Species Act, 29, 33, 140

Endeavor, 123

environment, 28–29
 human activity and, 49

environmental organizations, U.S., 29
 IRS and, 29

Everglades National Park, 25

"exotic" species, 141

exurban development, 45

F

Fiery Furnace, 47

Fletcher, H. D., 127

Florida, 25

flowers, sunburst anemone, 33

forest fires, 45

Forest Management Act, 19

Forest Reserve Act, 19

forest reserves, 19, 20

Forest Service, 22

Fort Baker Institute, 41

Free Niagara, 14

Fry, Dene, 123

FUNAI, 114

G

Gardner, James T., 14

Gateway National Recreation Area,
 32

General Land Law Revision Act, 19

Gettysburg, 18

Glacier National Park, 18

global interconnections, 141

global warming, 48

gold mining and miners, 110, 111–112

Golden Gate National Parks
 Conservancy, 40–41

Golden Gate National Recreation, 32

Golden Gate Park, 14

Grand Canyon National Monument,
 20

*The Grand Canyon of the
 Yellowstone*, 16

Grant, Ulysses S., 2, 16

grazing, 23

Great Barrier Reef, 5, 134, 135
 navigation and, 125

Great Barrier Reef Marine Park,
 119–135
 map, 122
 perceptions, 119
 tourism, 119, 126, 126, 130–131, 134
 tourist map, 124

Great Barrier Reef Marine Park
 Authority, 5–6

Great Blue heron rookery, 41

Greater Yellowstone Ecosystem, 141

Great Smoky Mountains National
 Park, 26

Green Party, U.S., 29

guns, 46–47

H

Habitat/Species Management Area,
 145

Haeckel, Ernst, 28

Harris, Judith, 149

Hartzog, George B. Jr., 32

Hayden, Ferdinand Vandeveer, 16

Hayman Island Resort, 127

Herculaneum, 83, 86, 92, 95
  skeletons, 89

herder and cattle, 77

Hetch Hetchy Valley, dam, 22

Hewett, Edgar Lee, 20

Hickel, Walter, 32

hiking, 47
  extreme, 46

Hill, David B., 14

Historic Preservation Tax Incentives, 29

Hoffman, Paul, 34

Hoover, Herbert, 26

Horonami Organización Yanomami, 115

Hot Springs National Reservation, 13

House of Julia Felix, 97

House of the Cryptoporticus, 89

Hutukara, 115

I

Ickes, Harold L., 26

Indian reservations, 10

International Labour Organization's Convention, Yanomami, 113–114

International Union of Conservation of Nature (IUCN), 141
  protected areas classification, 144–145

Ise, John, 17

Italy, 4–5
  Pompeii, 83, 86–97

J

Jackson, Andrew, 13

Jackson, William Henry, 16

Japanese-American sites, 39

Johnson, Robert Underwood, 18

K

Kekexili Reserve, 5

Kent, William, 23

kiang, 64

Kyoto Protocol, 141–142

L

Lacey, John F., 20, 21, 22

lama, 59

Lacey Act, 20

Land and Water Conservation Fund, 31, 33

land ownership, U.S., 141

Land Trust Alliance, 13, 44

land trusts, 10, 11, 13, 41, 44

landscaped parks, 14

Langford, Nathaniel P., 16

Latino sites, 35, 38–39

lawsuits, 29

legislation, 28–29

leopard
  Serengeti, 73
  snow, 63

Leopold, A. Starker, 28, 28

Leopold Report, 45, 139

Lincoln, Abraham, 15

livestock
  Chang Tang, 68, 68
  Serengeti, 73, 78
  U.S. parks, 23

lobbyists, 20

Loiyangalani archeological team in the Serengeti National Park, 81

Love, Rosaleen, 130

lumber companies, 22, 25

M

Maasai
  warrior, 77
  woman milking a cow, 78

Mabulla, Audax, 148

Mainella, Fran, 35

malaria, 112, 112
  inoculation, 112

Man and Nature; or, Physical Geography as Modified by Human Action, 27–28

Managed Resource Protected Area, 145

management, adaptive, 140

marine protected areas, 35

Marine Protection, Research and Sanctuaries Act, 31–32

Mariposa Grove, 15

Marsh, George Perkins, 27–28

Mather, Stephen T., 23, 23, 25

McCullough, David, 49

McFarland, Horace, 23

McKenzie, Col, 131

megalinks, 140

Mid-Kunlun Reserve, 5

military sites, 39
  national military parks, 18, 26

minerals, 111

Ministry of the Environment, 111–112

missiles, 39

Mission 66, 27

missionaries, 113

monasteries, Chang Tang, 68

Monterey Bay National Marine Sanctuary, 33

Montezuma Castle National Monument, 24

Moran, Thomas, 16

Mott, William Penn Jr., 35

Mount Shuksan, 31

Mountain States Legal Foundation, 33

Muir, John, 18–19, 22, 26

N

Naples, Gulf of, 86
  archeology, 83

National Environmental Policy Act (NEPA), 29

National Heritage Areas, 39

National Historic Preservation Act, 28

National Marine Sanctuaries, 31–32

national military parks, 18, 26

national monuments, 20
  administration, 22–23

National Oceanic and Atmospheric Administration (NOAA), 10, 31–32

National Park Act, 142

National Park Conference, 20

national parks, 2, 9, 21, 144–145
  administration, 22–23
  boundaries, 25, 45, 140–141
  defined, 144
  management, innovations, 44
  number of, 2
  system, growth, 36–37
  visitors, 27, 47–48

National Parks Association, 26

National Parks Conservation Association, 23

National Park Service (NPS), 11, 12, 18, 26
  establishment, 22–23, 25
  expanding visions, 36–37
  funding, 33, 142
  management, 34–35
  mission, 48
  role, 34–35

National Register of Historic Places, 27

National Trails System Act, 31

National Trust for Historic Preservation, 13

National Wilderness Preservation System Act, 28

National Wildlife Refuge Improvement Act, 34

National Wildlife Refuge System, 32, 34

Native American sites, 35

"natural," 28

Natural Monument, 145

Natural Resources Conservation Compliance Program, 10

nature, scientific understanding of, 139–145

networks, 140–141

New York, 13–14

Ngorongoro Conservation Area, 3–4, 71–81
  see also Serengeti

Niagara Falls, 13–14

Niagara Falls Association, 14

Niagara Reservation State Park, 14

Nixon, Richard, 32

North Carolina, 25, 27

North Cascades National Park, 31

North Dakota, 19

Northern Pacific Railroad, 18

Norton, Gale, 34

Noss, R. F., 140

NPS See National Park Service

O

Obama, Barack, 46–47

oil and gas
  Alaska, 32
  offshore leases, 31
  underwater, 29

Olduvai Gorge, Zinjanthropus find-site, 79

Olmsted, Frederick Law, 14

Olmsted, Frederick Law Jr., 23

Olympic National Monument, 22

Oplontis, archeology, 94

Organic Act, 23

P

Papāhanaumokuākea Marine National Monument, 35

Parima-Tapirapecó National Park, 113

parks. See national parks

Parks, Parkway and Recreation Area Study, 27

Parks Canada, 142–143

pastoralists, 65, 68

Maasai, 71, 73
  Tibetan, 60, 62
  Pelican Island, 25

pika, 61, 64–65

Pinchot, Gifford, 20, 22

plants, Chang Tang, 60, 61

poacher, 65

Pocock, Celmara, 151

Pompeii, 83, 86–97, 86–97
  archeological projects, 94–95
  bread, 92
  frescoes, 83, 90, 91
  funding, 90, 91
  management, 91–92
  mosaics, 92, 96

POMPEIVIVA, 90

Prairie Meadows Burning, 15

Preservation of American Antiquities, Act for the, 20

Presidio Trust, 44–45, 44

privatization, Niagara Falls, 13–14

protected areas, 2
  defined, 144
  private, 13
  region, by, 4
  variety, 3
  world, 3

protected landscape/seascape, 145

Pro Yanomami Commission, 113, 115

public lands, 17–18

Public Works Administration, 27

R

railroads, 18

Raymond, Israel Ward, 14

Reagan, Ronald, 33, 46

Rebozo, Bebe, 32

Reclamation Service, 22

recreation, motorized, 45–46

recreation areas, 27

Richardson, Henry Hobson, 14

Right of Way Act, 18

Robbins, William, 28

rock climbers, 46

Rockefeller, John D. Jr., 25–26

Rocky Mountain National Park, 22

Roman life, 86
  gardens, 86–87, 87, 88, ✖✦

houses, 87, 87
Roosevelt, Franklin D., 26
Roosevelt, Theodore, 19, 20, 26
Roughley, Theodore C., 126

S

"Sagebrush Rebellion," 33
Santa Fe Railroad, 18
scenic parks, man-made, 14
Schaller, George B., 147
Schwarzenegger, Arnold, 13
Sequoia National Park, 45
Serengeti
    Maasai, 77, 78
    villagers, 76
    wildlife, 73
Serengeti National Park, 3–4, 71–81
Serengeti Sopa Lodge, 79
shabono, 103, 104, 105
sheep, bighorn, 38
Sheridan, Camp, 17
Shiloh, 18
Sierra Club, 19, 22, 29
Smoot, Reed, 23
snorkeling, 127, 131
snow leopard, 63
Somma Vesuviana, 95
Southern Pacific Railroad, 18
sports, extreme, 46
Sportsmen's Heritage Act, 47
Stabiae, 94–95
state parks, 10, 11, 12–13
Stephenson, Nate, 139
Strict Nature Reserve, 144
stupa, 58
sunburst anemone, 33
Survival International, 113, 115

T

Taft, William Howard, 22
Tanzania, 3–4, 71–81

tax incentives, 29
Tennessee, 25
Theodore Roosevelt National Park, 19
Theseus the Liberator, 90, 91
Thomas, Michael L., 94
Tibet, 5, 51–69
    nomads, 58, 60
Tibetan snowcock, 61
timber, 22, 25
Timber Culture Act, 19
tourism
    Great Barrier Reef, 119, 124, 126, 130–131, 134, 126
    Pompeii, 90–91
    Serengeti, 78, 79
trails, 31
Trans-Alaska Pipeline. Alaska Native Claims Settlement Act, 32
Tripod with Satyrs, 97
Tweed, William C., 48

U

Udall, Stewart, 28
UNESCO, 2, 99
    biosphere reserves, 140
"unimpaired," 139
urbanization, 14
U.S., 2, 3
    area, 9–10
    Army, 17
    Department of Agriculture, 10, 20
    Department of Commerce, 10
    Department of Defense, 10, 11
    Department of the Interior, 9, 10, 21, 33
    Division of Forestry, 20
    federal and tribal lands, 9–10
    Fish and Wildlife Service, 9–10, 11, 34
    Forest Service, 3, 10, 11, 19
    funding, 33
    legislation, 19, 29, 28, 29, 31–32, 33, 140
    public lands, management, 9

usufruct rights, 114
Utah, 27, 38, 41, 47
Utilitarian Conservation, 19

V

Vaux, Calvert, 14
Venezuela, 99, 102 –117
    Conquista del Sur, 110
    rights, 115
Vesuvius, 83
    eruption, 86, 86, 93
Vesuvius National Park, 4–5
Via dell'Abbondanza, 89
Villa dei Papyri, 95
Voting Rights Act, 31

W

War Department, 18
Washington, 22
water, 22
Watson, Fiona, 150
Watt, James, 33
Weir, Joshua, 131
West Kunlun Nature Reserve, 5
Wild and Scenic Rivers Act, 28, 31
"wild" areas, 139
Wilderness Act, 27
Wilderness Area, 144
Wilderness Society, 27
Wildlands Project, 140
wildlife, 25
    Chang Tang, 55, 58, 59–60, 60, 61, 64, 64
    Serengeti, 73, 73, 76
    survey, 28
    U.S., 19
Wilson, Woodrow, 22
wolf, Chang Tang, 62
women's sites, 39
Wood, Nicholas, 87